HOLT Databank SYSTEM
A SOCIAL SCIENCE PROGRAM

William R. Fielder, General Editor

INQUIRING ABOUT
TECHNOLOGY

STUDIES IN ECONOMICS AND ANTHROPOLOGY

Mindella Schultz
Educational Consultant

Holt, Rinehart and Winston, Publishers

NEW YORK   TORONTO   LONDON   SYDNEY

Professor William R. Fielder, the General Editor of the HOLT DATABANK SYSTEM, received his Ed.D. in Elementary Education from Stanford University in 1960. Prior to his present position as Professor and Director, Division of Graduate Studies in Education, Oregon State University, he served on the faculties of San Jose State College, Stanford University, Michigan State University, and The Claremont Graduate School and University Center. He has acted as director of a number of educational research projects, including projects in differentiated staffing and instructional television, and has also served as a consultant to local and regional school systems. Professor Fielder is a co-author of *Social Study: Inquiry in Elementary Classrooms* (1966) and a contributor to a variety of professional journals.

Dr. Mindella Schultz, the author of *Inquiring About Technology*, is a graduate of Colby College with a major in economics and sociology. She received a Master's and Doctor's degree in Curriculum Development with a social studies emphasis from Carnegie-Mellon University. She has taught social studies and has worked with teachers to develop teaching strategies designed to involve students in educating themselves.

ACKNOWLEDGMENTS

The author expresses her gratitude to Veronica Geng and Susan R. Nevas for help in preparing these materials.

The author extends special acknowledgment to Yvonne R. Freund, in association with Karen J. Collidge and Anita Dickhuth, for photograph research.

Grateful acknowledgment is hereby made to the following authors, publishers, agents, and individuals for their permission to reprint copyrighted materials.

On pages 24–28, LOTHROP, LEE & SHEPARD COMPANY, INC. for adaptation from "Egyptian Symbol-Writing" from *Signs and Symbols Around the World* by Elizabeth Helfman, copyright © 1967 by Elizabeth Helfman. Reprinted by permission.

On pages 107–111, JOHN COLLIER and ANIBAL BUITRON for adapted excerpt from *The Awakening Valley* by John Collier and Anibal Buitron, copyright 1947 by John Collier. Published by the University of Chicago Press. Reprinted by permission.

On page 118, PRINCETON UNIVERSITY PRESS for "On the Farther Bank of Sava River . . . ," an excerpt from *Family in Transition: A Study of 300 Yugoslav Villages* by Vera St. Erlich, copyright © 1966 by Princeton University Press. Reprinted by permission.

On pages 122–123, 135, 136–139, RANDOM HOUSE, INC. and SECKER & WARBURG, LTD. for adapted excerpts from *Facing Mt. Kenya* by Jomo Kenyatta, published in 1962 by Random House, Inc. All rights reserved under International and Pan American Conventions. Reprinted by permission.

On pages 245–254, THE MACMILLAN COMPANY and JONATHAN CAPE, LTD. for excerpt from *Manchild in the Promised Land* by Claude Brown, copyright © 1965 by Claude Brown. Reprinted by permission.

On page 324, SCOTT, FORESMAN AND COMPANY for pronunciation key from *Thorndike Barnhart Junior Dictionary* by E. L. Thorndike and Clarence L. Barnhart, copyright © 1974 by Scott, Foresman and Company. Reprinted by permission.

Cover illustration by Richard Sparks.

Credits for art and photographs appearing in the textbook are given on pages 340–341.

56789   071   987654321

Contents

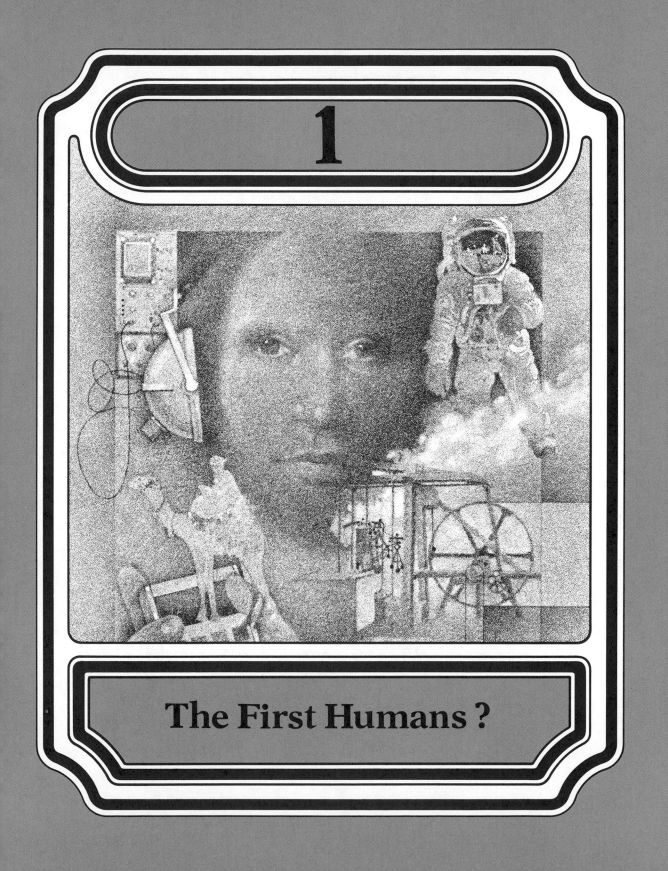

1

The First Humans ?

Was Zinjanthropus Human?

MARY LEAKEY FINDS SOME TEETH

"I've got him! I've got him!"

"Got what?" I asked.

"Him, the man! *Our* man," Mary said. "The one we've been looking for. Come quick. I've found his teeth!"

Magically my headache departed. I somehow
fumbled into my work clothes while Mary waited.

As we bounced down the trail in the car, she described
the moment of discovery. She had been searching
the slope where I had found primitive tools in 1931,
when suddenly her eye caught a piece of bone
stuck in a rock slide. Instantly she saw that it was part
of a skull—almost certainly not that of an animal.

Her glance wandered higher, and there in the rock
were two large teeth, side by side. This time there
was no question: They were surely human. Carefully,
she marked the spot with a pile of stones, rushed
to her Jeep, and sped back to camp with the news.

The trail ended half a mile from the site, and we
left the car at a dead run. Mary led the way.
I saw at once that she was right. The teeth had
belonged to a human. I was sure they were larger than
anything similar ever found, nearly twice as wide as
modern man's.

I turned to look at Mary, and we almost cried with sheer
joy, each seized by that terrific emotion that comes
rarely in life. After all our hoping and hardship and
sacrifice, at last we had reached our goal—we had
discovered the world's earliest known human.

LOUIS AND MARY LEAKEY DEVELOP A THEORY

Dr. Louis S. B. Leakey, a British-trained archeologist, wrote the account you just read. Archeologists study the remains of early humans. When Louis and Mary Leakey saw the teeth and the skull they were attached to, they believed that they had discovered the remains of a human being. They named their find *Zinjanthropus.*

They could not be sure they had discovered a human being until they had enough evidence to see if *Zinjanthropus* fit a definition of human. The Leakeys needed to define what a human being was first. To say

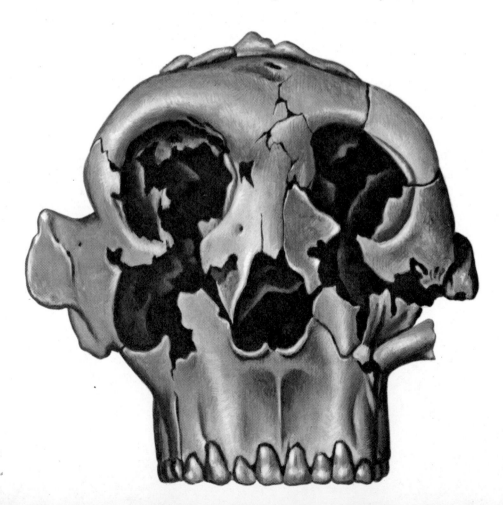

whether or not *Zinjanthropus* was human, they used this definition. A human being is a creature who makes tools in a regular, set pattern to be used for a particular purpose.

Looking at the Evidence

The teeth and skull of *Zinjanthropus* were found on a living floor that was over one million years old. A living floor is an ancient campsite where people made their home and left things behind them. On the cleared ground of this living floor, the Leakeys found piles of cracked bones. The bones looked like the remains of a meal made from small animals.

The Leakeys also found stone tools nearby. Stone tools look just like any other stones or pebbles. But Mary Leakey was an authority on stone tools. She could tell if a pebble was a tool. She was sure she had found tools on the million-year-old living floor. The tools were pebbles chipped away at the edge in a regular set pattern. The edge could be used for cutting or scraping. Mary Leakey guessed that the tools had been made to skin and cut up small animals for food. The Leakeys were sure that *Zinjanthropus* had made these tools. They were also sure that they had been made in a regular, set pattern to be used for a particular purpose. *Zinjanthropus*, the Leakeys thought, was human. The oldest human yet found.

Primitive hand axes on a living floor

Figuring Age

How far back in time do human beings go? To find the answer, archeologists study the bones of people and animals. Geologists study the rocks and layers of the earth where the remains of living things have been found. They can figure out the age of rocks and the layers of the earth. Using these methods, scientists discovered that *Zinjanthropus* was 1,750,000 years old!

Homo Habilis

Zinjanthropus was found in 1959. Two years later, working in the same area, the Leakeys found another skull and some finger and foot bones. Maybe this new creature was the toolmaker.

The Leakeys could tell from the foot bones that this new creature had walked upright on arched feet. The new creature had flexible hands that could have been used to make tools and skin animals. The teeth showed that the new creature was a meat-eater.

The Leakeys concluded that both *Zinjanthropus* and this new creature could have made the tools. However, they believed it was likely that the new creature was the more advanced toolmaker.

The Leakeys named their find *Homo habilis*. *Homo* is the Latin word that refers to human beings. *Habilis* means able and skillful. *Homo habilis* was skillful in making and using tools.

NEW EVIDENCE AND NEW CONCLUSIONS

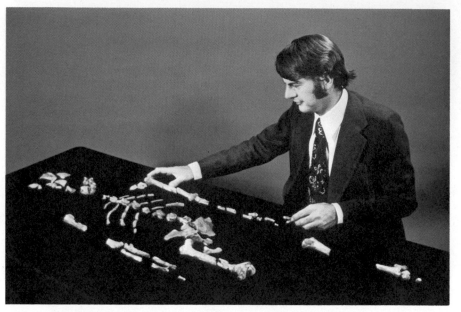

Dr. Donald C. Johanson examining fossils discovered in Ethiopia

The Leakeys' ideas about *Homo habilis* were still theories, just like their earlier ideas about *Zinjanthropus.* New evidence would change these theories.

Mary Leakey once said, "The situation is more complex than we dreamed." It became even more complex when some recent discoveries were made. One discovery was made by the Leakeys' son, Richard. In 1973 he found a skull in northern Kenya. Scientists believe that it is about 1 million years older than *Zinjanthropus.*

In 1973 and 1974 pieces of bone were found in Ethiopia. What is surprising about this discovery is that scientists believe that these pieces of bone were 3½ to 4 million years old! It seems now that early humans may have lived a lot earlier than anyone dreamed.

2

What Is Technology?

Something More

Early humans were wanderers. They were hunters. They moved from place to place in search of their food. Often their home was where they stopped for the night.

About 10,000 years ago, people stopped wandering and hunting for their food. They built homes. They grew food. They tamed animals to use for food and to help them do their work.

Nobody knows just when or why people stopped wandering. Some archeologists say that people settled near places rich with shells, or nuts, or metal, or wild animals, so they could trade these things to other people. Some say the first people to settle down were farmers, who accidentally dropped some wild seeds that took root.

Whatever the reasons, when people settled down their lives changed. Like *Homo habilis*, people made tools. But they also developed technology. Technology is tools plus something more. You will learn about technology and how it develops by studying people in ancient Egypt and people in Shang China.

Ancient Egypt

DESERT AND RIVER

A desert and a river—such was Egypt many thousands of years ago. Yet by 3000 B.C., people had made the desert and the river work for them. They changed Egypt into one of the first great centers of culture.

The quiet flooding of the Nile River during the summer months and the fertile soil of the Nile Valley made it possible for the early settlers of Egypt to develop a rich agriculture. Because of this, a large number of people could settle close together. Archeologists estimate that by 2000 B.C. the Nile Valley fed over 5 million people.

The Egyptians developed a technology that helped them to grow more food on less land and to do things people had not been able to do before. You can still see some of the results of their technology. The biggest stone buildings in the world are the pyramids of Egypt.

Tourists marvel at the pyramids, and engineers add them to lists of great engineering feats. But the Egyptians did not build the pyramids to surprise tourists or engineers. They built them to house the dead bodies of their rulers. The pyramids are tombs.

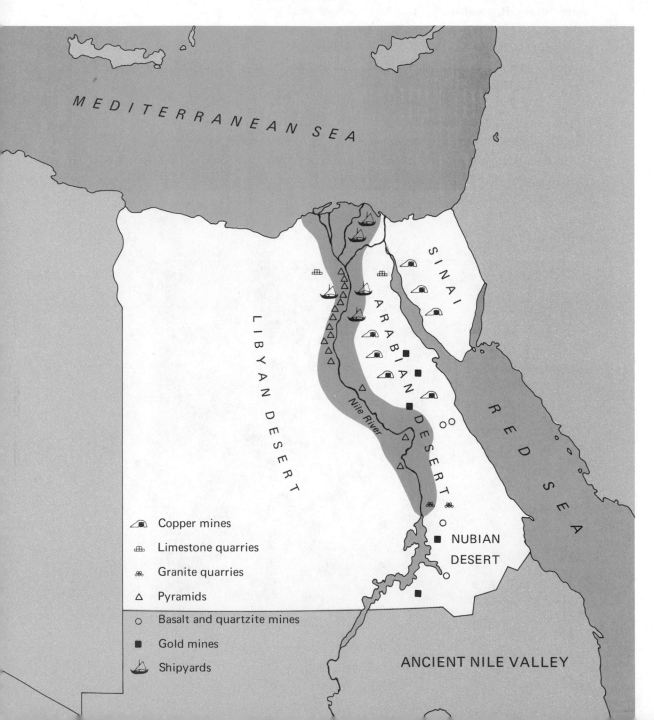

MEDITERRANEAN SEA

SINAI

LIBYAN DESERT

ARABIAN DESERT

Nile River

RED SEA

NUBIAN DESERT

⊿ Copper mines

⊞ Limestone quarries

⚒ Granite quarries

△ Pyramids

○ Basalt and quartzite mines

■ Gold mines

⛵ Shipyards

ANCIENT NILE VALLEY

First Tombs

The early kings of Egypt had been buried in simple flat tombs called mastabas. Made of mud brick, the mastabas were built far from the Nile's banks, so the summer river-flood would not wash them away.

Sometime around 2700 B.C., a king named Zoser asked his royal architect, Imhotep, to build him a tomb. Imhotep used stone instead of mud bricks. At first he built a regular mastaba. Then he changed his mind and made it square. Finally, he made it bigger by piling more mastabas on top of the first one, each smaller than the one below. The result was a pyramid of mastabas. From the side, it looks like steps. Because of this, people call it a step pyramid.

Some historians think Imhotep had a special reason for building the step pyramid. About that time, the Egyptians were adding a new idea to their religion: the idea that after death the king went to live with the sun-god. One of their religious writings said, "A staircase to heaven is laid for him so that he may climb to heaven thereby." Could the step pyramid have been a "staircase" to heaven?

Real Pyramids

Around 2600 B.C., the pyramid-builders got another idea. They did away with the "steps" and made pyramids that had slanting sides. No one knows exactly why they did this. But again, some historians think the reason has something to do with the sun-god religion. The rays of the sun shine down through the clouds at about the same slanting angle as the sides of these pyramids. Maybe the slanting sides of the pyramids stood for the rays of the holy sun.

The biggest and most famous of these pyramids is the Great Pyramid. King Cheops ordered it built for him. He wanted to top any pyramid built before or after him, and he did. Another king tried the trick of building his pyramid on higher ground, but few were fooled.

It took thousands of workers to build the Great
Pyramid. During the three-month flood season in
summer, when no one was able to farm in the valley,
some archeologists believe that as many as 100,000
workers worked on the Great Pyramid. The rest of the
year, about 4,000 people did the work. They replaced
workers with new people every three months. It is
estimated that it took the Egyptians 20 years to build
this one pyramid. They had to make and move
2,300,000 blocks of stone. Each block was usually
about 2½ tons, but some weighed as much as 16 tons.
Engineers still wonder how the Egyptians did it.

BUILDING WITH NUMBERS

The pyramid-builders had to measure the square base for the pyramid. They had to figure out how to make the sides of the pyramid equal. They had to cut the stone blocks even and straight. Supervisors had to keep track of thousands of workers—quarry and stone workers, haulers, toolmakers, and other laborers. They had to know how long the workers would take and what wages to pay them. Scribes recorded the number of stone blocks cut, hauled, and laid in place each day.

To help do these jobs the Egyptians used a number system. It looked like this:

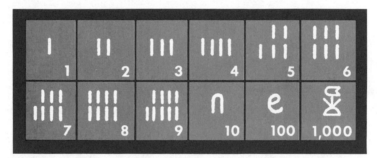

They wrote the number 43 like this:

How would you write 136 using Egyptian numbers?

Do you think the Egyptians could have done the jobs mentioned above without a system for counting and measuring?

LIVING WITH WRITING

Understanding Symbols

You are in a restaurant. You see two doors, with signs on them, like this:

Can you understand the signs?

You are at the Olympic Games. You see many signs to tell you where things are:

Do you know where to find the sport you like?

No matter what language you speak, you can guess what these signs mean. They are pictograms. Pictograms are symbols that picture real things.

Have you ever seen a traffic sign like this?

Or a wire fence with a sign on it like this?

Those signs are a little harder to figure out. They are ideograms. Ideograms are symbols that stand for an idea.

There is a third kind of symbol. You see a lot of them every day. Here are some samples:

These are phonograms. Phonograms are symbols that stand for sounds.

All three symbols—pictograms, ideograms, and phonograms—have been used in writing by different groups of people at different times. The following pages tell you how the Egyptians used symbols to write with.

Egyptian Symbol-Writing

The Egyptians developed a way of writing called "hieroglyphics." Hieroglyphic writing included many pictograms. Pictograms are simple pictures of things. But hieroglyphic writing was more than that, and it was much more complex.

Egyptian hieroglyphic writing probably began as real picture writing. Let's look at some of the signs:

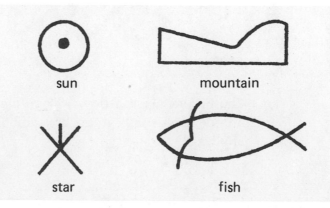

The fish looks like a fish. The star looks something like a star. The sun and the mountain might be hard to figure out. Once known, however, they would be easy to remember.

It is hard to make pictures of such things as the sky and water. This is how the Egyptians did it:

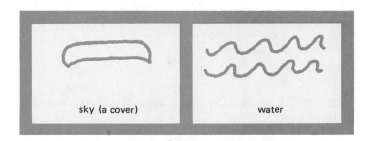

sky (a cover)   water

Written signs like the two above stand for not just the things themselves, but also the idea behind the things. When the sky is shown as a cover, the sign stands for the feeling of the sky. The Egyptians thought the sky was a cover over all the world, resting on the mountains on either edge of it.

The hieroglyph for "water" stands for its motion. How else could you make a simple picture of water?

Egyptian symbols were also put together to make new meanings. A closed flower under the cover of the sky meant "darkness":

The same sign with the addition of the sun low in the sky meant "evening":

The sky with a star or a lamp meant "night":

Water running down from the cover of the sky stood for "rain":

Action is also hard to show in written signs. The Egyptians did it by drawing something that you would naturally think of in connection with the action. Two legs meant "to go":

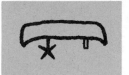

Two eyes meant "to see." Eyes with drops of water coming from them meant "to weep":

Sometimes the same hieroglyph, unchanged, could be both a pictogram and an ideogram. You have seen

that 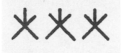 meant "sun." It also meant "day." A

"sun" is something that you can see and make a picture of. But "day" is something you cannot see. That is why it is an ideogram.

The hieroglyph for "star" sometimes stood for just the star of dawn. It also meant "to pray." Egyptians often prayed at dawn, when only a few last stars could be seen.

The plural for "star" was a picture of three stars:

✷✷✷

Other plurals were made in the same way. Three symbols stood for any number more than one.

Pictograms and ideograms were only part of hieroglyphic writing. Long ago, at the beginning of Egypt's recorded history, there were hieroglyphic signs that stood for, not things or ideas, but parts of spoken words. There were also about twenty-four signs that stood for single spoken sounds. These were phonograms.

Pictures of things, and idea-pictures, and sound-signs
were all used together in Egyptian writing. This was
complicated. And some hieroglyphs had several
meanings. Combinations of signs were often used to
stand for a single thing or idea.

The following combination meant "thirst":

The first two signs are letter-signs that stand for *ab,*
the Egyptian word for "thirst." To be sure this was
clear, however, the sign for "water" was added, and
following that, a man pointing to his mouth.

Why do you think the Egyptians developed
a system of writing? For what purposes do you think
they used it?

LIVING WITH MYTHS

The people of the Nile Valley who had once been wanderers learned to be farmers. In summer, the Nile overflowed its banks, spreading rich mud across the valley. The farmers plowed and sprinkled seeds in this fertile mud. The sunny weather did the rest. Crops grew rapidly. Sometimes the people harvested two or three crops a year.

Life was not this easy every year, however. Some years there was a "bad Nile." Rains fell too lightly to swell the river to overflowing. Or maybe too much rain fell. Then the Nile rose higher and higher, washing away houses, drowning men and cattle.

Over many centuries, the Egyptians worked out ways to deal with these problems. By studying the stars, they learned how to predict the weather.

Egyptian myths explained that Osiris was a god who once ruled the world. Osiris gave people knowledge about farming and made things grow.

Horus was Osiris' son. The Egyptians believed their gods could take the form of a bird or an animal.

They invented a calendar, using their number and writing systems to keep track of changes in the annual flooding. They figured out ways to build dikes, irrigation canals, and tanks for storing water. All this technology helped them deal with their problems.

Still, technology did not solve all their problems. Some years there was not enough water in the Nile flood. Other years there was too much water and there were disastrous floods. For help with their problems, Egyptians turned to their gods. They told stories about the power of their gods and about how people should treat the gods. These stories are called myths.

People use myths to explain events they do not understand. All peoples have myths. The myths of the ancient Egyptians helped them to explain their special problems and to know what to do about them.

Shang China

FROM EGYPT TO CHINA

Ancient Egypt was one of the world's first great centers of technology. Another great center of technology developed in Shang China. As you examine the art, number and writing systems of Shang China, ask yourself: How does technology develop?

Royal tombs, thirty to forty feet underground, are evidence of the technology developed by the people of Shang China.

"DRAGON BONE" CLUES

For hundreds of years, Chinese doctors gave their patients a special medicine. It was called "dragon bone" powder, and was made from ground-up animal bones.

In 1899 Chinese scholars happened to see a few of these bones. On the bones they noticed rows of carvings—tiny symbols and pictures. The scholars thought these markings were a very old form of Chinese writing. With horror, they realized that Chinese patients had been swallowing important evidence of ancient history—as carelessly as people today gulp aspirin!

Chinese legend says that the Shang dynasty ruled part of China from about 1700 to 1100 B.C. Since these rulers came from the same family, they are called a dynasty. But there was no proof of their rule—until the discovery of the "dragon bones." The scholars thought the writing on the bones was just about that old.

To get still more proof, they traced the bones to a place called Anyang, just north of the Yellow River in central China. A farmer there had turned up the bones while plowing and had sold them to a druggist.

Shang Cities

In 1928 archeologists began to dig at Anyang, looking for more evidence of the Shang dynasty. They got it. Under layers of earth, they found ancient tombs, thirty to forty feet underground. Buried there were beautiful, skillfully made carvings of wood and stone. There were marble sculptures and pottery. They also found bronze containers for eating, drinking, and cooking, and bronze parts of horse-bridles and wheeled chariots. They unearthed the remains of wooden houses, palaces, and temples.

Digging out stone post bases,
once a foundation of a house

The bronze objects found at Anyang were very beautiful. Their detailed designs could only have been made by people who knew complex methods of bronze casting. Workshops where bronze vessels were made were discovered in an even older Shang city at Chengchow. Chengchow was the capital of the Shang kingdom from about 1700 to 1400 B.C.

If you look at the following map, you can
find the borders of the Shang kingdom in its most
powerful days. The king collected taxes from all the
people in this kingdom.

Area controlled by Shang Dynasty

Reading the Bones

Archeologists use discoveries like pottery, carvings, and bronze pieces to recreate a picture of how people lived. If they are lucky, they may also find written evidence.

At Anyang, the archeologists were very lucky. They found a very special kind of written evidence: tens of thousands of "dragon bones," smoothly polished and carved with thousands of different symbols.

Why was this writing so special? Imagine that every day you wrote down a few questions that bothered you. They could be important questions about politics or religion. Or they could be everyday questions like whether you should play baseball or watch television. Think how much archeologists would learn about your way of life if they ever found your list of questions.

That is exactly the kind of writing that is on the "dragon bones." The symbols are questions that the Shang people asked their dead ancestors and their gods. The people asked for advice from their ancestors, who they thought were very wise. They asked the gods for advice too, for the gods were very powerful. If you pleased the gods, they could help you grow a good wheat crop or win a victory over an enemy. If you angered them, they could send armies to kill you, diseases to make you ill, or ghosts to scare you at night.

Scholars call the "dragon bones" by another name: oracle bones. An oracle is a person that predicts the future and gives wise advice.

Here is how archeologists think the oracle bones were used. If you wanted to ask a question, you went to the temple where the bones were kept. You told your question to a diviner, who was something like a priest. The diviner asked the question for you, and then selected a bone, usually the leg bone

of an ox, but sometimes a piece of tortoise shell. He heated the bone, causing it to crack. From the shape of the crack, he decided the answer to your question. Usually he wrote your question beside the crack and put the bone away for safekeeping.

At first, the Shang people used the bones only for very important questions. But after a while, they asked for advice on all sorts of everyday matters. Because of this, the writing on the oracle bones gives a clear idea of the problems the Shang people had and what their lives were like.

CHINESE SYMBOL-WRITING

Writing as an Art

Chinese writing has changed since the days of the Shang. Here is how the character for "sky" has changed:

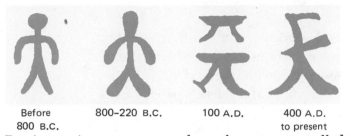

Before   800–220 B.C.   100 A.D.   400 A.D.
800 B.C.   to present

But in one important way, these characters are all the same. They are an art, like painting or music.

The art of writing is called calligraphy. In calligraphy, the shape of a character is just as important as its meaning.

Throughout Chinese history, great calligraphers have taught young students how to write. The first lesson is learning how to hold the brush: straight up and down—not slanted the way you hold a pen or pencil. Next, the students practice making brushstrokes, learning just how thick or thin they must be. Then they learn in what order to make the strokes for a character:

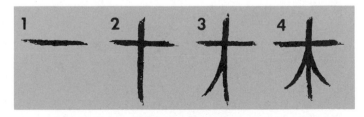

Chinese calligraphy requires a steady hand and an artist's eye. It also takes much time. Calligraphers have practiced patiently for twenty to forty years before mastering the art.

Shang Writing

Much of the Shang writing that is known today is on the oracle bones. But archeologists have found a few other examples, too. There are historical records telling about the rulers, their families, and their courts of nobles. There are records of payments— perhaps tax records. There are writings explaining how to construct a building.

From these historical records, it is known that the Shang government sent its armies written orders and made written treaties with its enemies. It is also known that at a Shang funeral, mourners carried a silk banner on which was written the names of the dead and the details of their lives.

Most of what is known about Shang China is written on bone, bronze, and pottery. Legend says that the Shang people wrote in books of bamboo and wood, but these have not survived. Can you think why?

CHINESE NUMBERS

The people of Shang China also had a number system. Can you think how they might have used numbers? Do you think numbers helped them to develop their technology?

Here is how the Shang people counted to ten:

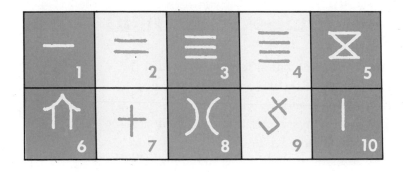

The number system developed by the Shang people was a good one. They were the first people who could write any number, however large, with no more than nine numerals. Here are some more of the numbers they used:

The Shang people wrote 88 like this:

And 656 was written like this:

How would you write 45 in Chinese? how about 352?

TECHNOLOGY = TOOLS + SOMETHING MORE

Ancient Egypt and Shang China were two of the world's earliest centers of technology. Their peoples had tools plus something more.

Technology solved some of their problems. It created other new problems that had not existed before. Most important, it changed the way people approached their problems.

3

Becoming Modern

What Is Modern?

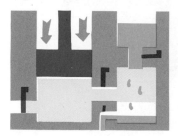

More than 3,000 years separate Shang China from the world of today. During those 3,000 years there were many changes. Some of the changes were small. Other changes were large. But, large or small, changes built on changes to make the world of today.

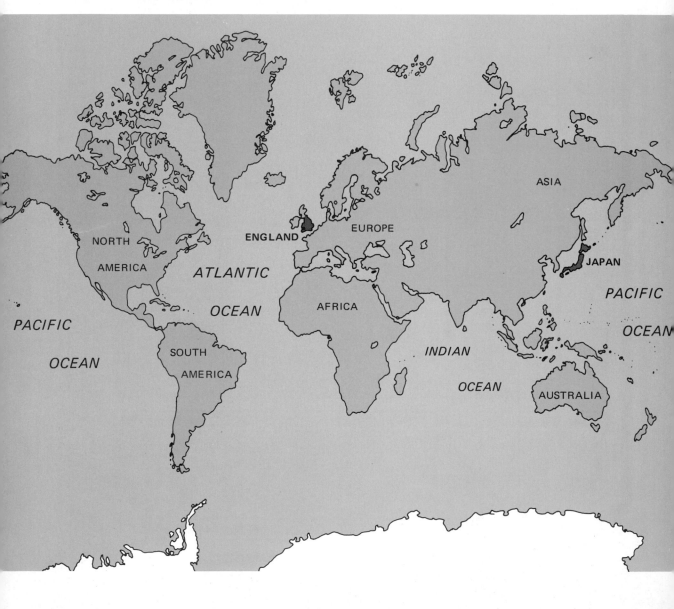

Many of the most important changes were in technology. Since the days of Shang China, people have added many tools, machines, and skills to their technology. These changes in technology have had an important effect on the way people live. To see how people's lives were affected, you are going to study two groups of people—the English and the Japanese. England was the first country to develop a modern technology. Today, of all the countries in Asia, Japan has the most modern technology.

Becoming Modern: England

THE STEAM ENGINE COMES TO ENGLAND

England has been becoming modern for hundreds of years. But before 1750, the changes were spread out over long periods of time. Then, suddenly, several changes happened within a very short time. Many of these changes were new machines. These machines either made new things or made old things faster or cheaper.

The opening of one of England's first railway lines

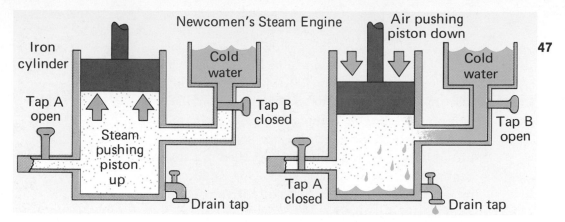

Newcomen's Steam Engine

Iron cylinder

Tap A open

Steam pushing piston up

Cold water

Tap B closed

Drain tap

Air pushing piston down

Cold water

Tap B open

Tap A closed

Drain tap

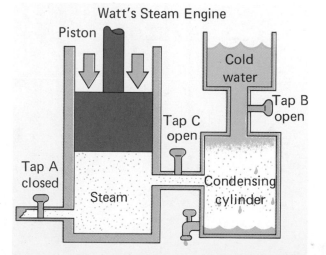

To start, Tap A was opened to let in enough steam to push the piston up. Then Tap A was closed and Tap B opened to let cold water in to condense the steam. Air then pushed the piston down. The water was drained and the process started again.

One of the new machines was an engine run by steam. In 1705 Thomas Newcomen invented a steam engine that could make rods go up and down. Sixty years later, James Watt was repairing a steam engine like the one Newcomen invented. Watt realized he could improve Newcomen's engine. He made a faster, more powerful steam engine that used less fuel. Compare the drawing of Watt's engine with the drawing of Newcomen's engine. Can you figure out why Watt's engine worked better?

When steam pushed the piston to the top of the cylinder, Tap A closed. Tap C then opened to let steam into a side cylinder. Air pushed the piston down. Tap B was opened to let cold water into the side cylinder to condense the steam. The water was drained and the process repeated.

Watt's Steam Engine

Piston

Cold water

Tap B open

Tap C open

Tap A closed

Steam

Condensing cylinder

Watt's steam engine, like Newcomen's, just made rods go up and down. It could be used only for jobs that called for an up-and-down motion, like pumping water. But Watt continued to experiment. By 1782 he had invented a way to make his engine turn a large wheel. That's why he called it a steam engine with rotary motion. His engine could now do more than power a pump. It could drive machines, such as spinning jennies.

Watt's invention was based on Newcomen's steam engine. It also built on earlier inventions and discoveries that made up technology. Watt's knowledge of tools and machines driven by human, animal, water, and wind power helped him when he invented his steam engine.

"Old Bess" was the first steam engine with rotary motion used at Soho mill. "A" is the steam cylinder, "B" the steam pipe, and "H" the condenser.

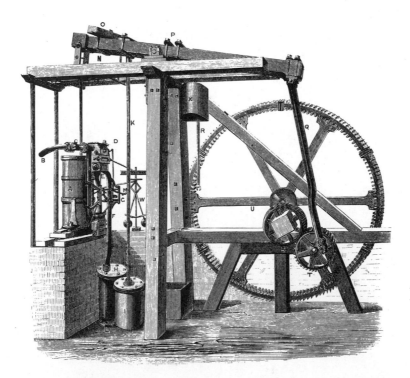

WHAT HAPPENED TO WORK?

Watt's new steam engine quickly made its way into the industries of Great Britain. By 1800 Watt and his partner had produced about 500 engines. The engines were used all over Great Britain.

Steam engines made important changes in one of England's biggest industries. Steam engines changed the way textiles were made. In the 1700's in England more people worked in textile making than in any other industry except farming. And almost everybody used the yarn and cloth made by the textile industry.

The use of steam engines in making textiles caused changes that affected a lot of people. By studying these changes, you can see what happened as England became modern.

Steam engines used in coal mining

Steam engines
used to transport
coal and to print textiles

Weaving.

Reeling Cocoons

Working in Cottages

In the 1700's, most textiles were made by people who worked at home. Because of this, textile-making was called a cottage industry. It often worked like this: A merchant collected the raw wool and delivered it to the spinners' cottages. The cottagers spun the wool into yarn. The merchant then collected the yarn and took it to the weavers' cottages. The weavers made the yarn into cloth. Finally, the merchant picked up the cloth and took it to small mills for finishing. There was no real clothing industry. Most families bought the finished cloth and made their own clothing.

Many cottagers were full-time spinners or weavers. Some farmers spent only part of their time making textiles. Spinners were usually women, while most weavers were men. A few cottagers had small workshops attached to their houses in which their families and a few apprentices worked.

Many of the textile workers were children. Sometimes, children were sent to "schools" to learn how to make lace and other special cloth. These schools were really workshops where children worked in cramped, dark rooms, often without pay. Here is a description of one lace school:

The hours were from 6 a.m. to 6 p.m., in the summer, and from 8 a.m. to 8 p.m. in the winter. Half an hour was allowed for breakfast and for tea, and one hour for dinner, so that there were ten hours for actual work. The girls had to stick ten pins a minute, or six hundred an hour; and if at the end of the day they were five pins behind, they had to work for another hour.

Steam engines and the machines they drove, like spinning machines, were too big and cost too much to be used in the cottages. And the cottagers' small machines could not compete with the fast new tools. By the early 1800's, textile-making was no longer a cottage industry.

Working in Mills

By 1815 most English textiles were made in large mills, where many spinners and weavers used new steam-powered machines. That year, Robert Owen, a millowner, visited some British factories. He took his fourteen-year-old son with him. Years later, his son described the tour this way:

We visited all the chief factories in Great Britain. The facts we collected seemed to me terrible almost beyond belief. We found that children ten years old worked fourteen hours a day, with but half an hour for the midday meal. It was eaten in the factory. In the cotton mills, they worked in temperatures usually hotter than seventy-five degrees. The air they breathed hurt their lungs because of the dust and cotton fibers in it. Some mills were run fifteen and sixteen hours a day with a single set of hands. And they employed boys and girls as young as eight years old. We found some even under that age. Most of the overseers openly carried leather whips, and we frequently saw even the youngest children severely beaten. In some large factories, from one-fourth to one-fifth of the children were crippled or hurt by too much work or punishment. The younger children seldom held out more than three or four years without serious illness, often ending in death.

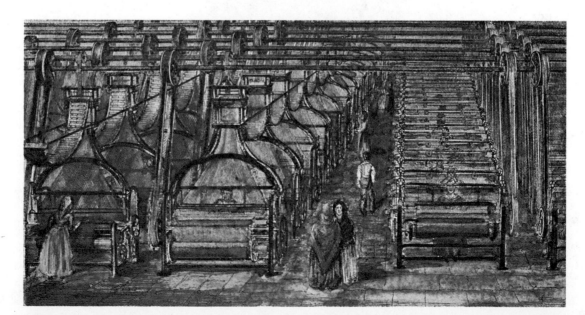

WHAT HAPPENED TO COMMUNITIES?

Working conditions were not the only part of life that changed for those who went to work in the new textile factories. Living conditions and communities changed, too. Here are descriptions of two communities. One description is of a cottage district. The other is about a factory district. Compare the two communities. How did living conditions change?

A Cottage District

Daniel Defoe is the author of *Robinson Crusoe.* He toured England in 1724. Later, he wrote about his travels. Here is his description of a cottage district in northern England:

From Blackstone Edge to Halifax is eight miles; and
all the way is up hill and down.

The nearer we came to Halifax, we found the houses
thicker, and the villages greater in every valley.
The sides of the hills, which were very steep, were
spread with houses.

In short, after we had mounted the third hill we found
the country one continued village. Hardly a house
stood out of a speaking distance from another. As
the day cleared up, we could see at every house
a frame, and on almost every frame a piece of cloth,
kersie, or shalloon; which are the three items of this
country's labor.

We found at every house a little gutter of running water.
If the house was above the road, it came from it,
and crossed the way to run to another. If the house
was below us, it crossed us from some other distant
house above it. These little streams were so guided by
gutters or pipes, that every house had one.

After using this water, the houses release it filled
with the dye, soap, oil, and other things used in the
making of cloth. The lands through which it passes
are enriched by it.

Every clothier must keep one horse, at least, to fetch
home his wool and his goods from the market, to
carry his yarn to the spinners, his cloth to the mill, and
when finished, to the market to be sold. Everyone
also keeps a cow or two for his family.

We saw houses full of workers, some at the dye-vat,
some at the loom; the women and children carding or
spinning. All were employed from the youngest to
the oldest.

An early ironworks disrupts a country scene.

A Factory District

The following report is about living conditions of working people. It is part of a report made in 1842 by a government official.

It is impossible to give a proper picture of the bad conditions of many of the poor class on the streets of Pipewellgate and Killgate. Each small apartment contained a family with seven to nine lodgers and seldom more than two beds for the whole. The writer, a short time ago, visited a person ill of the cholera. His lodgings were in a room of a miserable house. The house was divided into six apartments and occupied by different families numbering 26 persons in all. The room contained three beds with two persons sleeping in each. It measured about 12 feet in length and 7 in width. Its greatest height would not let a person stand up straight.

WHAT DID THE ENGLISH THINK?

The English people talked and wrote about the changes caused by the new machines. Workers, writers, artists, and lawmakers were some of the people who praised or criticized the new way of life caused by steam-powered machines.

The Luddites

Some workers fought the machines and the factory system. They feared that the machines would take away their jobs. The new machines could produce more goods with fewer people. Many hand craftspeople were also proud of their work. They feared that their reputation for fine work would be lost.

In 1811 the stockingmakers from Nottinghamshire went from factory to factory smashing knitting machines. They were called Luddites because they claimed that their leader was named Ned Ludd.

The Luddites spread to other parts of England and to other trades. In 1812 weavers began to smash power looms. The Luddites often sang or chanted as they destroyed machinery. One of their favorite songs went like this:

Around and around we all will stand
And sternly swear we will.
We'll break the shears and windows too
And set fire to the mill.

Strikes

Many workers realized that smashing machines could never bring back the old ways. They demanded higher wages and better working conditions. Their usual method of protest was to call a strike.

One early strike took place in Manchester in 1810. The strikers wanted higher wages. They stayed away from the factories for four months, but the owners refused to meet their demands. Most workers had to return at the old rate of pay while some got even lower pay.

Most early strikes were unsuccessful. This was mainly because the laws made unions illegal. In England at this time, most of the laws were made by people who owned the factories and the land. Workers did not have the right to vote. As more and more people began to work in the factories, they demanded that they be represented in the government. After many years, they gained the right to vote and a political party, the Labor party, was formed to speak for them.

Even though unions were illegal, some unions were formed anyway. But because they had to meet secretly, they stayed small. Small unions could not organize large strikes, and factory owners could easily find new workers to take the places of a few strikers.

In England the laws against unions were done away with in 1824. But it was not until the 1850's that workers had enough support to begin to form strong unions. They got people to join their unions by holding meetings, making speeches, and singing songs. Here is one of the songs they sang:

It's high time that working men should have it their own way,
And for a fair day's labor, receive a fair day's pay.

The working men, by thousands, complain their
fate is hard,
May order mark their conduct, and success be
their reward.

Employers must be made to see they can't do
what they like,
It is the master's greediness causes the men
to strike.

Our London Weavers mean to show their masters,
and the trade,
That they will either cease to work, or else
be better paid.

Other Ideas

Many English people wrote about the new factories. Some, like Charles Dickens, were shocked by the way children were treated. In books like *Oliver Twist,* he tried to describe the problems of factory workers and their families. Other writers did not share Dickens' views. For example, W. Cooke Taylor, wrote these thoughts:

We no longer think that inventions take away jobs and food from the poor. Jobs in every branch of industry have increased because of machines. We know now that every new mill creates new jobs.

Child labor is a question of meat, drink, and clothing. How are the children to be supported without their earnings in the factories? If children were not given jobs in the mills, it is not quite clear what would become of them. Their homes could not contain them. They would be out in the street with all its temptations. Juvenile labor may be bad but juvenile delinquency is worse.

The jobs that children have in the factories are not hard. But they are boring and tiresome. Time for recreation and instruction is certainly necessary in the factories.

The children in the mills are better off than most poor children in England. The mill is a better place than the mine, the ship, the forge, and very many private workshops.

I go further, and state that if a system of child labor did not exist, it should have been the business of the nation to create it.

OVER POPULATION

Laws

People in government also disagreed about the new factories. Some felt that working and living conditions were no worse than they had ever been. Furthermore, the new factories provided jobs for the landless, unemployed poor.

Others thought that the factory system took advantage of the workers. In 1802 a factory law was passed. Here are some of its terms:

All rooms and apartments belonging to any mill or factory shall, twice in every year, be well and completely washed with quick lime and water over every part of the walls and ceiling. Mills and factories must provide enough windows and openings in such rooms for a proper supply of fresh air.

No apprentice shall work for more than twelve hours in any one day. No apprentice shall work between nine o'clock at night and six o'clock in the morning.

Becoming Modern: Japan

THE STEAM ENGINE COMES TO JAPAN

In the middle of the 1800's, the way people lived in Japan was a mystery to the people of most countries. For more than two hundred years, the Japanese government did not allow foreigners to enter the country. It also did not allow Japanese people to leave the country. The government did not want the Japanese people to come in touch with the views of people from other countries.

By 1850 several countries wanted to open Japan to trade. As nations built up their industries, their factories made more goods than they could sell at home. They needed new markets. They also wanted to see what Japan might have to sell to them. In 1853 American ships entered Tokyo Bay.

Although most Japanese wanted to make the foreigners leave the country, the government quickly saw that the American military force was too strong. The Japanese government refused to fight. A new government came to power in 1868. But even it could do nothing. However, the leaders of the new government were determined that Japan would never again have to bow before foreigners. Japan must develop military power, they decided. Military power meant becoming modern.

So the Japanese set out to make their country modern. They had a strong base on which to build. Japanese craftspeople were highly skilled, particularly in metal working. In 1850 almost half the people in Japan were able to read and write. This was higher than most European countries.

The government helped build up Japan's industry. They gave people willing to start factories loans to buy new machinery. Japanese students were sent abroad to learn modern business methods. The steam engine and other new machines came to Japan.

Kyoto, about 1700

Many foreign companies set up offices in Japan. An example is this office building used by the English.

These new machines changed the old ways of making and doing things. The making of silk in Japan in 1850 was like the early making of textiles in England. It was a cottage industry. Farm girls pulled one thread at a time from a cocoon and spun it around a frame turned by hand. When Japan decided to become modern, the government sent people to other countries to learn about making silk. The Japanese built research laboratories, training schools, and factories. They used machines that spun many threads at once. At first, these machines were powered by water, then by steam, and then by electricity.

Once they could produce huge amounts of silk, the Japanese had to think of ways to get it to the people who would buy it. To do this, they built ships, trains, and trucks. Today Japan leads all nations in shipbuilding.

Before Japan became modern, iron and steel products were made in small workshops. Iron and steel began to be manufactured in giant factories and in huge amounts as Japan became modern. All sorts of products made out of iron and steel began to be manufactured by new machines.

The new machines did more than change the old ways of making and doing things. The Japanese people also started to make many new products. They learned how to make things like chemicals and plastics. Today, Japan ranks first in the world in the making of radios and television sets. It is third in the making of steel.

LIFE BEFORE THE STEAM ENGINE

In 1846 about 87 out of every 100 people in Japan were in farmer families. Wealthy landowners, scholars, and police were the next largest groups. About 8 out of every 100 people were in these groups. About 3 out of every 100 were in merchant families. The craftspeople, such as metalworkers and carpenters, were the smallest group. About 2 out of every 100 worked at crafts.

Once a person was born into one of these groups there was little chance of switching to another one. A son was expected to follow his father's occupation or one planned for him by his family. A daughter was supposed to live a life just like her mother's.

To learn about how people lived before Japan modernized, you are going to see how a farm family lived in 1850. Every member of the family had to help with the work. Farm communities were small, and most farmers knew their neighbors.

The homes of Japanese farmers were simple. To western eyes, even the homes of the wealthiest Japanese would have looked small and lightly furnished. But the Japanese saw beauty in simplicity. They preferred to keep their lives simple and orderly.

A Farm Family in 1850

The Matsui family lived in a farming village near the coast. Seven people lived in the small house: Hajime, the father; Hanako, the mother; their three children; and Hajime's old parents.

Family life was very important to the Japanese. There were a few simple rules which nearly everyone followed. For example, Hajime and Hanako's marriage had been planned by their parents. The couple had no part in the decision. They had known each other as children growing up in the same village. But, sometimes, when marriages were planned by parents, a young couple would meet for the first time at their own wedding.

Hanako's parents had been pleased by the match. Hajime was an eldest son and would someday own his family's farm. A farmer's eldest son inherited his land and was expected to take over

the work of the farm. Other sons were not forgotten
in the family. A second son could expect to find
a job on his family's farm or to receive help from
his family to start out on his own. Sometimes a
younger son would marry into a family that had only
daughters. Then he might be adopted as the eldest
son. One day he would own the family's farm.

The only occupation open to Hanako was
that of wife and mother. It was the only one
considered right for women. Hanako was a good wife
and mother. She helped with the farm work, kept
a neat house, and cooked the meals for seven people.
Most important of all, she raised three children
who obeyed their parents. They would care for her
and Hajime in their old age just as she and Hajime
were caring for Hajime's parents.

Hanako was glad when Hajime's mother no longer gave her so many instructions. When she was first married and went to live with her husband's parents, the older woman ran everything. Of course, Hanako had to obey her mother-in-law. Fortunately, her husband's parents liked her. If they had not, they might have forced Hajime to leave her. He would have had to obey.

Life had been good to Hanako. Hajime was a good husband and a successful farmer. There was a fine farm for their son to own some day.

Whenever another family suffered from a fire or flood, Hanako and Hajime were among the first to go and help repair the damage. They were well thought of by their village neighbors. This would help when it came time to plan good marriages for their two daughters. Hanako was teaching her daughters how to care for a household and how to act toward one's husband and mother-in-law.

Hanako believed that her family was happy because they did everything that was expected of them. They remembered and honored their ancestors; the young obeyed the old, and the women obeyed the men; they lived simply; and they were generous and helpful to their relatives and their neighbors.

LIFE IN MODERN JAPAN

In Japan today, most people are no longer farmers. More than half of Japan's people now live in cities or suburbs. Many people who live in the suburbs travel back and forth to the city every day to work. Many of these people hold jobs with large companies or the government. The Japanese call them salary workers. The number of salary workers in Japan is increasing. They make up a large part of the country's growing middle class. The following pages will help you to see how a salary worker and his family live in Japan today.

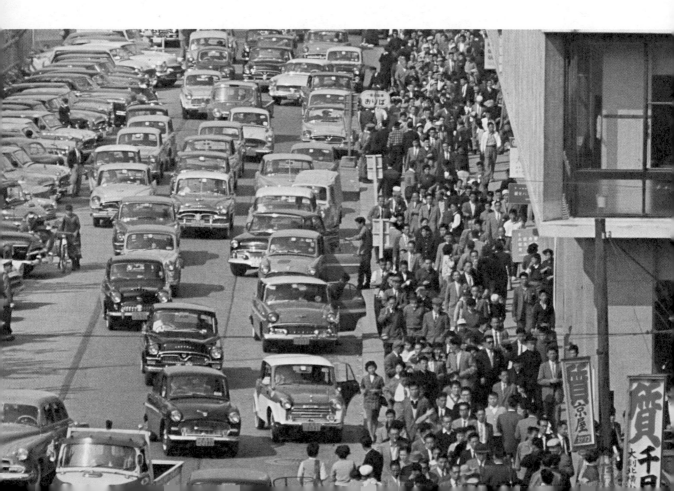

A Middle-Class Family

The Kodama family lives in a suburb of Tokyo. Their house is not large, but only four people live there: Jiro, the father; Aki, the mother; and their ten-year-old daughter and seven-year-old son.

The house, like the houses near it, is one story high. The Kodamas have furnished it with a mixture of older Japanese and modern western style furniture. Aki particularly likes the machines that save work, such as the electric rice-cooker and washing machine, in her kitchen. One of her neighbors has an all-electric kitchen.

Jiro is a salary man. He is a lawyer for a large company. His company makes and sells electronic equipment.

Jiro's father was a farmer. Because Jiro was a second son, his parents expected him to work on the family farm and to marry into a family that had only daughters. He would then become the adopted son of his wife's family. But Jiro had other plans. He did well in school and went on to a university. When he graduated, he found work with his present company.

Jiro has done well with his company and is very loyal to it. He would never think of working for another company.

Every morning, Jiro pushes his way into a
crowded train and rides for almost two hours to
get to work. When his work day is over, he usually
spends some time in the city with friends from

his company. Sometimes they go out to eat or they play a game of chess. Jiro gets home late, after the children have gone to bed. He does not see his children often during the work week. But he has Saturday afternoons and Sundays off, and he spends this time with his family.

Aki is proud that her husband is a successful salary man, but she really does not know much about his work. Jiro believes that work and family should be kept separate. He does not talk with his wife about his work.

Aki grew up in Osaka, a large Japanese city. She went to college and, for a while, considered becoming an airline hostess. Her parents did not like the idea. They believed that Aki should not look for a job since she would probably marry soon. Aki agreed and her parents began trying to arrange a marriage for her. Her parents were surprised when she turned down several marriages they had planned. Her marriage to Jiro was arranged by her uncle. Aki would not have agreed to the marriage if she and Jiro had not liked each other.

Aki spends part of every day cleaning,
shopping, and cooking. She thinks it is important
to keep her home clean and neat. Aki also manages
the family budget. But her most important job is
taking care of the children. They are in school most

of the day, but when they are home Aki takes them
with her wherever she goes. She helps them with
their homework. She wants them to do well in
school and hopes they will be able to go on to college.

The children are well-behaved and Aki hopes that they will not grow up to be disrespectful like some of the older children in the neighborhood. Aki does not talk to Jiro about them, because the children are her business. But sometimes she worries that her children will not obey her.

Aki does not like to have anyone help her with her housework or with her children. She is glad that she and Jiro have a home of their own. Some of the neighbors live with their parents because houses are costly and hard to find. Some parents, Aki knows, still believe in complete obedience, even from their grown children.

Aki and Jiro don't see their parents very often. The last time they visited Jiro's parents was three years ago and Aki's parents visited them a year ago. Aki and Jiro used to wonder how they would care for their parents when they got old. But now the government has taken over some of these duties. Their parents can get medical care and other help from the government.

Aki's life centers around her home. Sometimes she visits with her neighbors, but they don't help each other or share things with each other. Jiro has never met some of their neighbors.

Sometimes the children make trips to famous places with their school class. On weekends, the whole family often goes out together. They may go to the movies, visit relatives, or go to a baseball game.

The Kodamas like many things about modern life, but they are happy that some of the old customs are still used. They hope that the old ways will not be completely forgotten.

The people of Japan enjoy some of the old customs of their country by taking part in the above festivals.

OLD WAYS OR NEW?

There is great disagreement among the Japanese about whether the changes that have made a new Japan are good or bad. Some Japanese try to find the best in both the old and the new ways. But many young people are impatient with the old ways. And many older people still believe that the old ways are best. They find many parts of modern life unpleasant.

More and more young people in Japan are
beginning to disagree openly with their elders about
the importance of family loyalty, obedience,
worship, and government. Japanese students are
demanding greater freedom. They want to plan their
own education. Many young people no longer value
a simple life. They want western food, music,
and entertainment. They want all kinds of goods,
such as cars, television sets, and stylish clothing.

Many older people are shocked by the actions of the young. One older person from a big city expressed this feeling: "Today's young people are soft. They have never known hardship of any kind. They are loud and rude."

Japan has become modern. The way of life in Japan has changed. But its people still question whether the old ways or the new ways are best.

4

Nonmodern People

Who Is Nonmodern?

Think of all the different groups of people in the world. It is hard to think of so many millions of people. How were you thinking about them just now? Maybe you thought about them by the names of the countries or continents they live in: French people, English people, Mexican people;

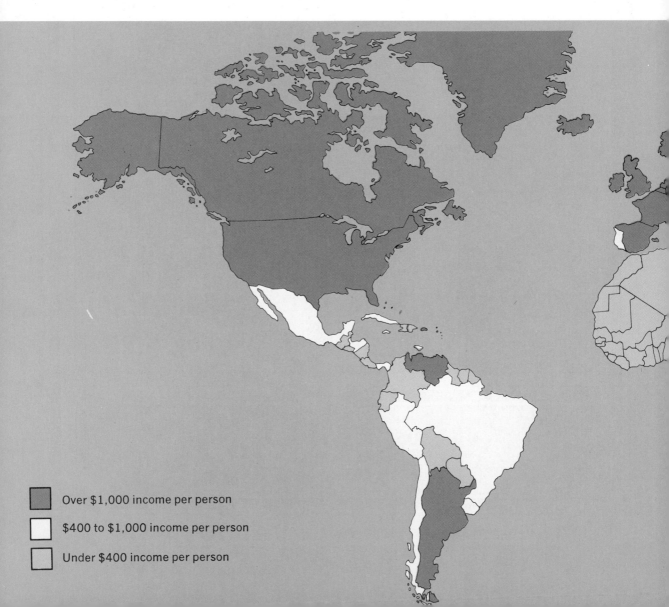

■ Over $1,000 income per person

□ $400 to $1,000 income per person

□ Under $400 income per person

Asians and Africans and Americans. Or maybe you thought about them by age: children and grown people; babies and old people.

Look at the map. How was the person who drew the map thinking about them? The next page shows the information on the map in another way. Look at it after you have thought about the map.

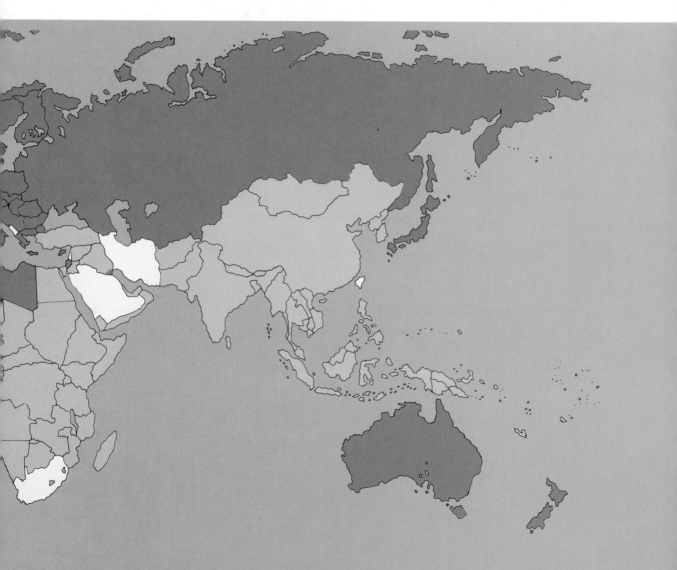

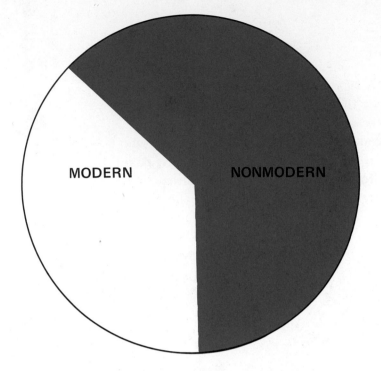

The circle stands for all the people in the world. Some are modern. But two-thirds of all the world's people are nonmodern. That is another way of thinking about all the people in the world.

People show whether they are modern or nonmodern by the way they live. The food people eat and the clothes they wear give clues to whether they are modern or nonmodern. Where people live gives you clues, also. It helps to know whether they live in houses or huts or tents or apartments. How people teach their children is important, too. Although most of the world's people are still nonmodern, their way of life is disappearing.

You are going to study three groups of nonmodern people—the Quechua-speaking Indians of Peru and Ecuador; Yugoslavian villagers; and the Kikuyu of Kenya. As you study, you will find ways to answer the questions: Who is modern? Who is nonmodern?

The Quechua

THE QUECHUA THEN

Quechua is not the name of a tribe or a place. It is the name of a language spoken by millions of people.

Quechua was the language of the Incas—a people who once ruled a powerful empire in South America. They built beautiful cities and strong fortresses of stone. From their capital city of Cuzco, they spread out, conquering millions of people from other tribes. They taught them to speak Quechua.

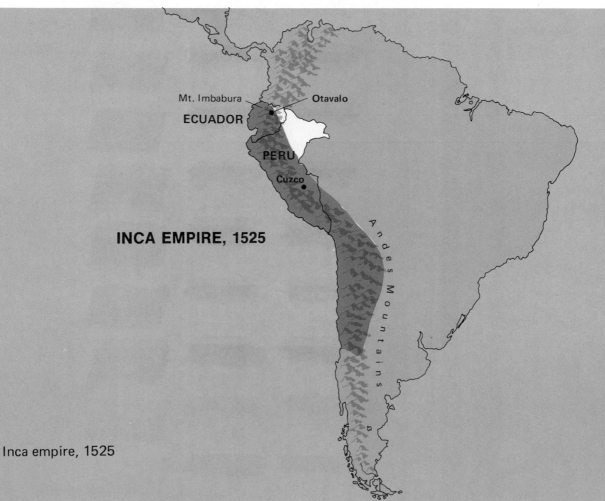

Mt. Imbabura   Otavalo

ECUADOR

PERU

Cuzco

Andes Mountains

INCA EMPIRE, 1525

Inca empire, 1525

People in other parts of the world were busy with conquest, too. Some of them ventured to South America. The Spanish came to the empire of the Incas. They had guns and fast horses. The Incas had neither. In 1553 the once-mighty Inca empire fell to the Spanish.

Even when Spain no longer ruled its South American colonies, the Spanish kept hold of most of the power and the land. The Indians were left to farm a few tiny plots of land or to work on the big Spanish-owned mines and farms for a small wage or share of the crops.

STRANGERS

Many of the Quechua Indians live around the old Inca capital of Cuzco, Peru. If you went there to see how they live, you would have to climb for hours into the high peaks of the Andes Mountains. The land there is poor and rocky. The Spanish left it to the Indians, keeping the richer lowlands for themselves.

If you went there, you might have a hard
time talking to the Indians or visiting their homes.
One writer, doing research for a book about Peru,
had this experience.

There were times when I met a group of Indian peasants on a lonely road when neither of us spoke, nor smiled, but seemed only to quicken the pace to put between us as fast as possible as wide a distance as we could. We both felt as if we belonged to different worlds. We knew we could not communicate with each other on the same wavelength.

After an earthquake that hit Peru in 1970, many Indians hid from the teams of rescuers and doctors, even though they needed medical aid. They were afraid and suspicious of people from outside their community.

The Quechua Community

To these Indians, the word community has a special meaning. Imagine that you lived in a place where your family had lived for hundreds of years. Next door to you and your parents and brothers and sisters lived your grandparents, and their brothers and sisters; your aunts and uncles, and all their children; all the brothers and sisters of your aunts and uncles; and so on. That would be a lot of people, and all part of one huge family. A Quechua community is made up of a few of these huge families. Young men and women usually marry someone from the community and they stay there to raise their children. These huge families have lived together as long as the oldest grandfather can remember, and even longer.

Sometimes, however, people from other places settle in the community. In one Quechua community, two girls married outsiders who had moved there. After living there for twenty years, these unfortunate bridegrooms were still being called "men without a place," outsiders forever.

In another community, a man sold his land
to a stranger and moved away. No one speaks to
the stranger. At planting and harvesting times, his
neighbors help each other, but he is left to struggle
alone as best he can.

The Quechua Family

One reason the community holds together is that so many of the people in it are related to one another. Parents give some of their land to their children when they marry, and those children later divide their land among their own children. After a long time, of course, the plots get smaller and smaller. Some sons are forced to leave their family land and go to work on big farms along the coast. To the Indians, working on one of these haciendas is not as good as working their own land.

The main job of everyone in a family with land is farming. Little children, two and three years old, go to the fields with their parents. They try the jobs their fathers and mothers do. If the family has a few sheep or llamas, the tiniest children herd them. They take turns so that some can stop to play. Older girls teach the littler girls how to spin yarn for cloth, weave baskets, or make pots out of snakelike coils of clay.

Few of the children go to school. The ones who do often speak only Quechua and cannot understand the teacher's Spanish. Not many schools have teachers who speak Quechua.

At the end of the day, the families gather in their huts. Everyone is glad to be together after

the long day's work. The children must be quiet
and respectful to their parents, but with their
grandparents they are allowed to joke and tease.
They surround the lively old people, laughing and
acting silly until it is time to eat dinner and go
to bed. Then long sleeping-platforms are spread with
woolly llama or sheep pelts and the family snuggles
under them to keep warm through the chilly
mountain night.

NEW QUECHUA WAYS

One of the tribes the Incas conquered was the Cara of Ecuador. The Incas forced them to give up their Cara language and speak Quechua.

Today, many of these Indians still live where their ancestors lived in Inca times—in Otavalo, Ecuador, on the slopes of Mount Imbabura. Here they grow maize, potatoes, and cabbage, and raise chickens. They live much like other Quechua Indians, but their lives are changing. The following account tells about some of these changes:

Change in Otavalo

Thirty years ago a white landlord asked an Indian near Otavalo to weave him a length of woolen cloth for a suit. The Indian, who had never woven anything but ponchos and native woolens, set up his loom and with great skill copied a sample of English tweed. The white man was delighted. Now he would not have to send all the way to London for material for his suits. He told his friends. They, too, ordered cloth. The original weaver shared his orders with a friend, and the foundation for a new business was laid.

Before the Otavalos began commercial weaving, they lived entirely by their land, farming only to eat, weaving cloth only to wear and to trade for goods required by them. Their land was barely able to support their subsistence economy. They had no source of cash with which to buy more land other than small earnings from local haciendas.

Now the Indians of Otavalo have a chance to make money without working far from home or toiling on the local haciendas. A primitive farming culture has been changed into a manufacturing and trading economy. Money profit for the Otavalos makes it possible to buy more land.

One might expect that communities having little land, or the least fertile land, would dedicate themselves to industry and commerce. On the contrary, the communities which have the most fertile land are the most industrialized or have developed commerce to the greatest extent. This is explained by the fact that land, more than anything else, gives independence, time, and money to the Indian. Only if he has land is it possible for him to acquire the loom, the raw materials, and the training necessary to produce cloth.

The Textile Industry

The textile culture of the Otavalos goes back to the earliest history of the Andean Indians. Before the coming of the Incas, the Otavalos and Indians of other tribes in Ecuador were weaving blankets and cloaks from cotton they obtained from the people of the Amazon jungle. The backstrap loom that served them then is still in use today in the making of blankets and ponchos.

Soon after the arrival of the Spanish in America the Indians were making use of two looms: the native backstrap and the broad Spanish loom. Today nearly all the Indians of Otavalo know how to weave. But the weavers fall into two distinct groups. Some weave only their necessary clothing, but others weave for sale in the market. The first group uses almost exclusively the native loom. The second group uses

A father weaves a poncho on a backstrap loom, while his son cards wool for spinning.

both native and Spanish looms. The first group weaves only ponchos and flannels. The second group weaves European-style woolen goods, blankets, shawls, heavy cotton goods, *fachalinas,* and belts as well. The first group spins by hand, a task only for women, using a spindle made of a thin and fragile reed. In the second group, both men and women spin, using a wheel which speeds up the process by at least five times. The first group weaves the wool in its natural colors. The second group is familiar with many kinds of dye.

The Otavalo Indian is undoubtedly one of the finest weavers of the Andes. The products of his looms are sought in all the markets of the country.

In the Indian home everyone works—men and women, children and old people. For each there is a task: washing the wool, drying it, picking out the burrs, beating it with a flexible rod to loosen the bits of dirt, carding it to straighten the fibers, spinning, winding the yarn into skeins, dying it, washing it, and drying it again. When the wool has been spun and dyed, the men of the family begin their work, warping the loom and weaving. Under the porch of the weaver's home all these activities go on at once. The husband may be weaving a section of poncho, a rectangle of flannel for a woman's skirt, or a length of European-style goods, while his wife spins a new pile of wool, and beside her the children pound up dye or card and wind up balls of wool.

Yugoslavian Villagers

WHO IS A YUGOSLAVIAN?

Yugoslavians have a saying about themselves:

We have: 1 country
          2 writing systems
          3 languages
          4 religions
          5 nationalities
             and
          6 republics.

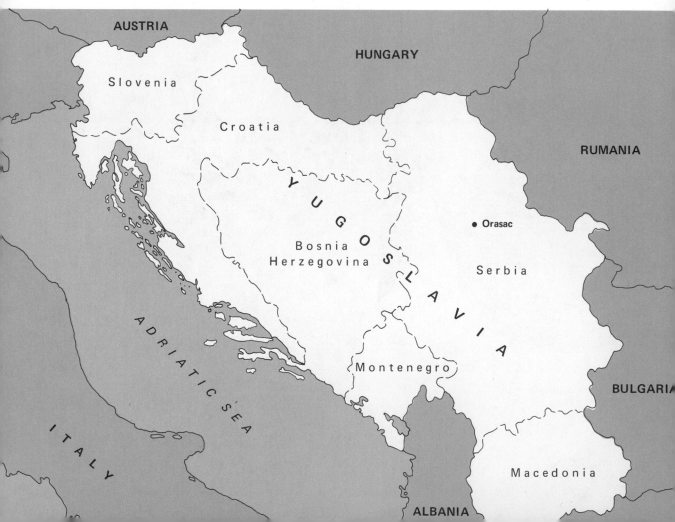

In 1918 the different writing systems, languages, religions, and nationalities were joined into a single country—Yugoslavia. And the country was divided into six official republics that are something like the states of the United States.

The people, however, continued to write, speak, go to church, and follow customs in their own special ways. So there is no such thing as a "typical" Yugoslavian.

However, more than half the people of Yugoslavia have at least one thing in common. They live in the country rather than in the city.

Here is something else that country people
have in common. Their way of life is changing. The
changes differ from place to place, but they touch
the old ways of life in almost every country village.

ONE OLD WAY: FAMILY FARMS

In 1962 in the village of Orasac, Serbia, the local lignite mine closed down. (Lignite is a soft coal used for fuel.) Until then, many villagers had used their wages from the mine for extra money. They added it to the money they made from their family farms.

In the past, Orasac farmers had cleared forest and pasture land to make new farmland. Now there was little forest and pasture land left. It cost more and more to live, but farm families were not getting more and more crops from their land. Many of the younger men began to leave the village for jobs in the nearby market town.

Yugoslavians were leaving their farms more and more each year. Many of them went to work on big government-run farms where machines had replaced sickles and ox-drawn plows. Others went to the cities to do factory work, returning to their village farms every night or on weekends. After a time, many of these workers sold their farms and moved into city apartments.

ANOTHER OLD WAY:
THE ZADRUGA

For hundreds of years, most Yugoslavian country people lived in a type of family called the *zadruga*. A man never left his family's home. When he married, his wife came to live with his family. The oldest man in the home—perhaps a grandfather—headed the *zadruga*. He governed the *zadruga*, although the other married men took part in making decisions.

While the men did most of the heavy farm work, women helped with the planting, weeding, hoeing, and fruit-picking. They also cooked, cleaned, made the family's clothing, and minded the children. But for all this work, they had little rank in the *zadruga*. There was a saying that a newborn baby boy ranked higher than the oldest grandmother. One observer asked a Yugoslavian woman how many children she had. "Two," she replied. He later learned that she had five, but that the three girls did not count. In some places, women had to stand while their husbands sat at dinner. And only a few women learned to read or write.

Life for Yugoslavian women is still hard. But as the old way of doing things breaks down, women's lives and their place in the family are getting better. The song on page 118 can give you an idea of what life in the *zadruga* was like for women.

On the farther bank of Sava river
Three young maidens dance the kolo,
In the chain is pretty Mara,
And this is what that maiden says:
Is there any of my kinsmen
To take my message to my mother
Never to give my sister's hand
To any man who lives alone,
But to marry her as I was,
Where the company's big as here,
With mother and with father-in-law,
With brother and with sister-in-law
Where husband has many sisters.
When I go to see my mother
Mother-in-law makes me a cake,
Daughters-in-law prepare my satchel,
Sisters-in-law deck me with beads,
Make me feel queen of the world,
See me gladly on my passage.
When we reach the village outskirts
Hang my satchel on my shoulder,
While I stand with satchel ready,
Cluster loving all around me,
Sending greetings to my mother,
Then upon my tender cheeks
Young wives, young girls plant their kisses
And, returning to the homestead,
Lingering eyes watch me depart.

Today, the old-style *zadruga* is almost gone. In some villages, like Orasac, parents and children usually still share their homes with grandparents and grandchildren, but the strict rules of the old *zadruga* are no longer followed.

A wedding picture

A peasant couple window-shopping

THE ORASAC COMMUNITY
The Clan

The old life of the village is almost gone now. But traces of the old village community remain for those villagers who have stayed on in Orasac.

Orasac villagers can trace their ancestry and find out which households belong to their clan. Often they can name every member of the clan, even someone living in another part of the village. When people meet for the first time, one of their first questions is, "Who do you belong to?" They mean, "What clan are you from?"

Clans are like huge families. Clan members go to each other's weddings and funerals. Each clan has its special saint, and on that saint's day, the clan gathers for feasting and dancing.

The Neighborhood

In Orasac, neighbors are usually members of the same clan. This makes for close neighborhood ties. But even with *komsija*—neighbors who are not members of the same clan—relations are very friendly. "A neighbor is closer than one's shirt," the people say. One Orasac villager told an American studying the village:

If you are in trouble or need anything you go to your *komsija* . . . sugar, kerosene for your lamp, a hoe or a sickle, even a little money.

Neighbors are often invited to weddings and parties, and very close neighbors may come to the saint's-day celebration of the clan. Neighbors also help each other with farm tasks and with other work. In spite of change, the people of Orasac are still close to their clans and neighbors.

The Kikuyu

LEARNING TO BE A KIKUYU

In the beginning of things, when mankind started to populate the earth, the man Gikuyu was called by the Mogai (the Divider of the Universe), and was given his share of land with ravines, the rivers, the forests, the game and all the gifts that the Lord of Nature (Mogai) granted mankind. At the same time Mogai made a big mountain which he called

Kere-Nyaga (Mount Kenya). He then took the man Gikuyu to the top of the mountain of mystery, and showed him the beauty of the country that Mogai had given him. While still on top of the mountain, the Mogai pointed out to the Gikuyu a spot full of fig trees, right in the center of the country. After the Mogai had shown the Gikuyu the wonderful land he had been given, he commanded him to descend and establish his homestead on the selected place.

In those words, Jomo Kenyatta, a member
of the Kikuyu tribe and first president of Kenya,
retells a legend about the beginnings of his tribe.
Kenya is a country of many peoples—mostly Africans,
a few Asians, Europeans, and Arabs. The Kikuyu are
the largest of the more than 40 African tribes in Kenya.
And they still live, as the legend tells, near Mount
Kenya in the center of the country, not far from
Nairobi, Kenya's modern capital.

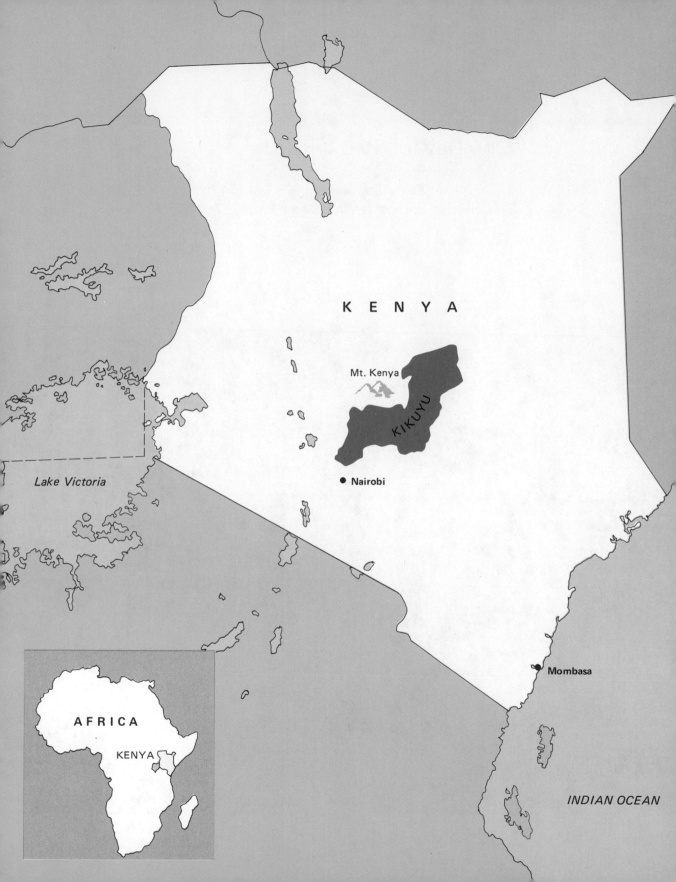

One Day for Two Kikuyu

One Kikuyu boy and one Kikuyu girl live
on a hillside in their family's two huts.

One hut is for the mother and daughter.
Inside, it looks like this:

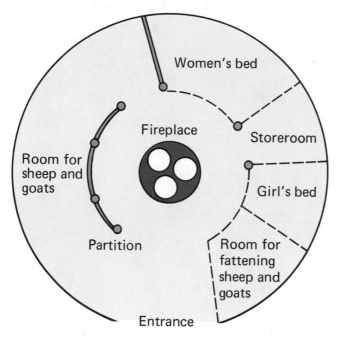

The other hut is for the father and son.

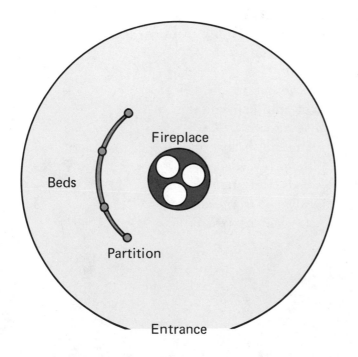

When the boy was a baby, he slept in his mother's hut. Now he is old enough to sleep in the men's hut where his father and other villagers gather to talk.

The two children call each other *moro wa maito* and *mware wa maito*—"son of my mother" and "daughter of my mother." They call their mother *maito* and their father *baba*. They speak to them in a quiet, polite tone to show respect. The parents, in turn, speak gently to the children.

Baba is the head of the household, while *maito* is the one who feeds and looks after the children. When the children were babies, she took them to the fields each day. She set them under a tree and tied a big bunch of leaves over their heads so the sun would not fall on them.

Now, the children wake up soon after dawn, go outside to wash, and then eat breakfast— perhaps a stew of vegetables from the family farm. The leftovers are wrapped in leaves for lunch. Then the children have jobs to do.

The girl goes with her mother to the fields. There she gets a small corner of land and imitates her mother's work with the hoe or knife. She weeds or harvests the rows of maize, beans, and sweet potatoes. At first, the little girl weeded out strong plants along with the weeds. But after a while she learned which was which. Now she is proud of her small garden and plans a feast at harvest time.

She also watches her mother do the housework. She gets her own pile of corn to grind and makes clay pots which she uses to play house.

The boy does not spend much time around the house. Those jobs are considered "woman's work," and no woman would want a man who could do them. They would call him *kihongoye*—"nosey."

Instead, the boy goes to the field with his father, especially at planting time. He copies the way his father uses a wooden digging stick to turn the soil. Some days he sits in a tree, scaring birds away from the crops.

The boy learns all about the plants and fruits and flowers. He learns which ones are poisonous and which ones can be eaten. His father explains these things to him on their long walks together.

The boy also has another job and a very important one. He is in charge of herding the family's goats, sheep, and one cow. These animals are as important to the family as money in the bank. The cow supplies a little milk and butter, and the goats and sheep are used for meat.

Herding is not all work. The boy meets other young herdsmen. They keep one eye on their animals to make sure they do not wander, get stolen, or attacked by other animals. With the other eye, the boys attend to their games: fighting, asking riddles, trying to ride an extra big billy goat.

One day, the boy returned with the herd. A little later, he met his father.

"Are all the animals back?" asked his father.

"Oh, yes," said the boy.

"Let's go take a look." They went over to the herd. "Hmm, I don't see the brown goat with the white spot on its leg."

The boy's heart thumped in his chest. Surely that goat had come home with the rest!

His father spoke gently. "Think back carefully. When did you see that goat last?"

The boy thought. He pictured the herd in his mind. He could see that goat. "Right before I met you, *baba*," he said. "It was standing next to the big black billy goat."

His father touched his shoulder. "You are right," he said. "I hid that goat to test your memory. You are getting to be a good herdsman."

The boy was very happy that his father was pleased. But he made up his mind never to answer quickly that the herd was safe—not until he had looked it over to be sure.

That night, the family gathered for supper. Usually they spent this time telling stories and legends and playing word games. For the children, this was fun. For the parents, it was a way to teach the things a grown Kikuyu had to know.

Tonight, however, was special. *Baba* announced that he was going to bring a second wife into the family. She would be able to help the children's *maito* with the farmwork and housework. *Maito* was looking forward to having someone to keep her company, too. And of course, with the new wife there would be new brothers and sisters.

The children were very excited. Friends of theirs had a second mother, too. They called her *maito munyinyi*—"little mother"—and loved her very much. That night, the girl dreamed of her new "little mother." The boy lay with his eyes wide open, listening to his father and some other village men talking around the fire.

BUILDING A KIKUYU HUT

The children's *baba* decided to build a new hut for his new wife. This news excited the children very much. A Kikuyu hut must be built in one day. According to tradition, evil spirits may move into the hut if it is left unfinished overnight. Many friends, neighbors, and relatives come to help build the hut, and a big party is held for them.

To prepare for building day, everyone first went out to gather materials. The men cut wood for the walls and poles, while the women gathered grass for the roof. People too old to do this work cooked food for the building-day feast.

Meanwhile, the children's father chose a spot for the hut. He made some beer from sugar cane, and on the morning of building day, sprinkled it on the ground to be used for the hut.

When the helpers arrived on building day, they first cleared and leveled the ground. Then the father put a stick in the middle of the area where the hut would be built. He tied a string to the stick and, holding the string tight, he walked around in a circle to mark the foundation of the hut. All the men helpers started digging holes along the edge of the circle to hold the wall. When the wall was up and the wooden roof was put on, the men's work was finished. They went off to feast and sing songs about building. They directed a few sarcastic songs at the women who were still working busily, putting grass on the roof:

Look on those lazy-bones who are working like chameleons, the sun is going down, do you want us to make torches for you?

The women replied:

You men, you lack the most important art in building, namely, thatching. A wall and an empty roof cannot protect you from heavy rain, nor from burning sun. It is our careful thatching that makes a hut worth living in. We are not chameleons, but we do thatch our huts like *nyoni ya nyagathanga* (a small bird known for its sweet songs and the neatness of its nest).

When the thatching was done, the women too joined the feast.

THE KIKUYU AND THEIR LAND

A Kikuyu Tale: Mogo wa Kebiro and His Prediction

Once upon a time there lived in Gikuyuland a great medicine man known as Mogo wa Kebiro. His national duty was to predict future events and to advise the nation how to prepare for what was in store. We are told that early one morning the prophet woke up trembling and unable to speak, his body covered with bruises. His wives on seeing him were very frightened. They did not know what had happened to their husband who had gone to bed in perfect health the previous evening.

Soon Mogo wa Kebiro regained his power of speech. With his usual prophetic voice he began to tell what he had experienced the previous night. During his sleep, Ngai (God) had taken him away to an unknown land. There Ngai had revealed to him what would happen to the Gikuyu people in the near future. On hearing this he was horrified. In trying to persuade Ngai to prevent the evil events coming to the Gikuyu, he was badly bruised and exhausted. He could not do anything but obey Ngai's command to come back and tell the people what would happen.

In a low and sad voice he said that strangers would
come to Gikuyuland from out of the big water.
The color of their body would resemble that of a small
light-colored frog and their dress would resemble
the wings of butterflies. These strangers would
carry magical sticks which would produce fire. These
sticks would be very much worse in killing than the
poisoned arrows. The strangers, he said, would later
bring an iron snake with as many legs as a centipede.
This iron snake would spit fires and would stretch
from the big water in the east to another big water
in the west of the Gikuyu country. Further, he
said that a big famine would come. This would be the

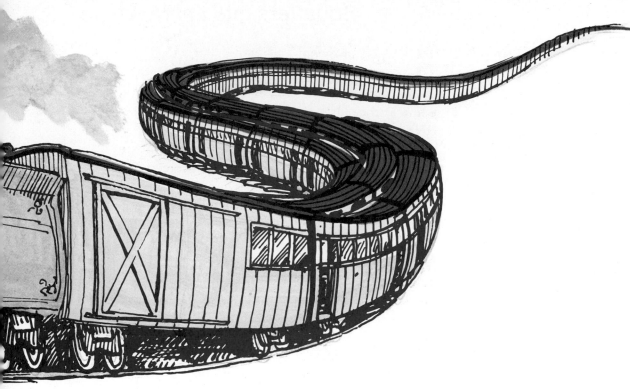

sign to show that the strangers with their iron snake
were near at hand. He went on to say that when
this came to pass the Gikuyu, as well as their
neighbors, would suffer greatly.

The great medicine man advised the people that when
these strangers arrived it would be the best policy
to treat them with courtesy mixed with suspicion.
Above all, they must be careful not to bring them too
close to their homesteads, for these strangers are
full of evil deeds and would desire the Gikuyu
homeland. In the end, they would want to take
everything from the Gikuyu.

Squatters into Landowners

Around 1890 the British came to the land of the Kikuyu. They declared the area under British rule. They built a railroad from Mombasa to Nairobi. Some Europeans stayed. They settled on the White Highlands around Nairobi.

When European settlers began to cultivate farmland in the White Highlands, they forced most of the Kikuyu onto a reserve—something like the Indian reservations in the United States. Some Kikuyu went to Nairobi to work at low-paying jobs. Still others became "squatters" on European farms. They cultivated a few acres for themselves, and in return for the use of this land, they worked for the European farm owner a certain number of days each year.

In 1937 one European, a Danish woman, wrote a book about her coffee farm. She described the fate of the Kikuyu squatters when she sold the farm to another European:

As the people who had bought the farm were planning to take up the coffee-trees, and to have the land cut up and sold as building-plots, they had no use for the squatters. As soon as the deal was through, they had given them all six months' notice to get off the farm. This was bewildering to the squatters for they had believed that the land was theirs. Many of them had been born on the farm, and others had come there as small children.

They asked me where they were to go.

The Natives could not, according to the British

law, buy any land, and there was not another farm
that I knew of, big enough to take them on as
squatters. I told them that I had myself been told that
they must go into the Kikuyu Reserve and find land
there. They again gravely asked me if they should find
enough unoccupied land in the Reserve to bring all
their cattle with them? And, they went on, would
they all be sure to find land in the same place, so that
the people from the farm should remain together, for
they did not want to be separated?

When Kenya became independent in 1964, its
government began to buy back European farms. The
government resettled Kenyan farmers on this land.

Subsistence Farming
into Cash Farming

Most of the Kikuyu, as well as other Kenyan
Africans, were subsistence farmers. They grew some
things to sell at the market, but mainly they farmed
to support their families.

The yield per acre on subsistence farms is
small. To increase the yield you need big farms where
big machines can be used. You need irrigation. You
need fertilizers. Subsistence farmers cannot afford
modern technology.

The government helps the farmers. When farmers buy young tea plants from the Tea Authority, they are shown how to prune the bushes and how to pick just the top two leaves and a bud so they will get the best tea. When the crop is harvested, farmers can take it to a government collecting station. The tea will be processed and sold for the farmers at an auction in Nairobi.

The government also started a training school to teach people how to operate tractors and other farm equipment, and how to run large farms of from 200 to 5,000 acres. Many students take the course each year. Many of them will manage cooperative farms bought by groups of Africans.

Farmers in a pyrethrum field. The flowers of the pyrethrum plant are ground up and used as an insecticide.

Nairobi's central business district

City and Country

Because the Kikuyu are the largest tribe in Kenya, and because they live near Nairobi, they hold many modern jobs. Much of Kenya's business, industry, and government is located there. But even these city people have ties to the land. Many of them still have farms in their home villages or are buying land on the outskirts of Nairobi.

Jomo Kenyatta has said that agriculture is the key to Kenya's growth and to a better life for its people:

I love the soil, and I love those who love the soil. The soil has knit us together. It is our greatest investment. By investing in the soil, one invests in lasting, long-term property. Other things come and go, but well-cultivated soil remains. The soil has been there from the beginning of time. Soil is the mother of wealth, development, and general prosperity.

5

A Changing World

A Stranger Comes to Tepoztlan

It is hard to be a stranger in a new place. Strangers may see things they have never seen before. Strangers see people whose names and ways of doing things are new to them. Strangers are outsiders. Only later, when they know the place well, do they begin to see it from the inside, like the people who live there.

A stranger is coming to Tepoztlan, a village in Mexico. The stranger is an anthropologist—a professional people watcher. Anthropologists are scientists who study the way people live. Watch along with the stranger and try to see what the stranger sees.

The stranger flew to Mexico City. From there, he took a bus into the mountains. Now the bus approaches the village of Tepoztlan, still hidden from the stranger's eyes by the surrounding hills.

Suddenly he sees an opening ahead in the wall of hills. The bus passes through and he gets his first look at Tepoztlan. There are small cornfields, separated from each other by low walls of rocks.

The stranger has a glimpse of houses, low and flat-roofed. They are almost hidden among the thick leaves of the trees.

Finally the bus rolls to a stop. The
modern road that connects Mexico
City with Tepoztlan ends here, at
the village plaza. The stranger gets
off the bus and looks around the
plaza. On one side is a park. He sits
down to rest on one of the park
benches and looks at the buildings
around the plaza.

One of the buildings near the plaza
is the central church. It is the tallest
building in the village.

Now the stranger is rested, and he
takes a walk through the village. Some
of the steep streets are paved with
stones.

Other streets are dirt paths, scattered with weeds and rocks.

The stranger passes some houses
made of a sun-dried clay called
adobe. Many seem to have just one
windowless room. The only opening
is a door leading to the yard. Trees
overhang the houses and the street.

Passing by, the stranger hears the sounds of people
talking and children playing. But no one speaks
to him. He is separated from the people of Tepoztlan
because he is a stranger.

AN ANTHROPOLOGIST LOOKS FOR CHANGE

One reason the stranger, the anthropologist, came to Tepoztlan is because it is changing. He is a people watcher, but he is not just interested in people as they are today. He wants to know what they were like in the past and what they might be like in the future. He is interested in change.

Dr. Oscar Lewis was an anthropologist. He first went to Tepoztlan in 1943 and then went back many times. Each time he returned to Tepoztlan, he noticed how it changed.

One way that people change is by becoming modern. Modernization brings people new tools, new ideas, new ways of life. For instance, you saw how new machines and new ways of doing things changed the lives of the English and the Japanese. Part of this change was the new things the people had. Anthropologists, like Dr. Lewis, call the things people have material culture. They use material culture to measure change. If an old thing is replaced by a new thing, that is a sign of change.

When Dr. Lewis first went to Tepoztlan to study its material culture, he was a stranger. But after a while he got to know the people and to see Tepoztlan from the inside.

Lewis studied and wrote about the people of Tepoztlan. Many of his studies tell about a peasant he called Pedro Martinez. He interviewed Pedro and his family, stayed with them, and kept records of what they did each day. He observed their material culture and noted what new things were added to it. He wanted to compare their past and present material culture. That way he could find out how new things changed the way they lived. But to do that, he had to learn about Tepoztlan's history and its past material culture.

Material Culture

Tepoztlan: The Past

TEPOZTLAN UNDER THE AZTECS

Quauhtli was an Indian boy. He lived in Tepoztlan where his father and his father's father had been born. These Indian men were important. As members of the village council, they helped rule their people.

Everyone expected that when Quauhtli grew to be a man, he too would help rule Tepoztlan. But something happened that changed Quauhtli's future.

The Aztecs, a tribe of powerful Indians, began spreading out from their capital city of Tenochtitlan. Tenochtitlan is now Mexico City. Ruled by a king named Montezuma, Aztec warriors took village after village into their empire. In 1437 they conquered Tepoztlan and sent Aztec lords to govern it. The village council lost its power. Quauhtli would not grow up to be a village ruler.

Reconstruction of Tenochtitlan

The lives of the villagers changed when the Aztecs came. Quauhtli and his father had always farmed a plot of land owned by the village. They grew corn and beans for food. Around the edges of the field, they grew cotton for cloth. But under the Aztecs, they also had to farm the fields of the Aztec lords. And as part of the Aztec empire, they had to give some of their own crops to the Aztecs. They had to work twice as hard with their digging sticks and hoes.

From May to October was the rainy season. It was good for farming. Then, at harvest time, Quauhtli's father carried the corn and beans and cotton from the field to their adobe house in the village. He put the crops into a basket and balanced the basket on his back. He held it there with a forehead strap called a tump line.

Quauhtli's mother, Tula, and his sister, Omechtli, stayed at home, but they worked just as hard. Using a stone metate, they ground corn which they made into tortillas. They picked the seeds out of the cotton, beat the cotton with sticks to make it fluffy, and spun cotton fibers into thread. Then they wove the thread into cloth. They made some of the cloth into clothing for the family. But they also had to make clothes for the Aztec lords and give them bolts of cloth to send back to Tenochtitlan.

Clay incense burner

Stone showing sun's role in Aztec religion

Double bowl

Aztec
Artifacts

Stone metate

Pottery vases and pitcher

Carved greenstone warrior

Vase with a figure of the god of song and dance

During the dry months, Quauhtli helped his father make charcoal from the trees in the forest. Sometimes he thought he would like to learn to make paper from the bark of the trees. He had watched the workmen in the village as they boiled the bark, washed it, and pounded it flat with heavy stone clubs. If he could make paper, he could take it to Tenochtitlan. There, in the marketplace, he could trade it for an Aztec bow and arrow or a spear.

Quauhtli did not get to Tenochtitlan, but he did go to the marketplace in Tepoztlan. He and his father went once a week. There he saw boys who came from nearby villages with their fathers. Some of them brought pottery, honey, sugar, and rope to the

45.

market. They carried their goods in baskets on their backs. Quauhtli and his father brought their extra cotton and corn and beans. Sometimes they agreed to trade one item for another. Sometimes they used cocoa beans for money.

Quauhtli worked hard, learning to be a man. He knew that when he grew up, he would have a field to work, a family to feed, and an Aztec lord whose fields he would have to work.

THE COMING OF THE SPANISH

An Aztec Prediction

Strange events began to happen in Tenochtitlan around 1500. A temple caught fire and burned for several days before the flames could be put out. The lake around the city rocked and heaved, sending flood waters into the city. Comets flew across the sky, and one very bright comet hung in the sky for days. Aztec priests studied these wonders. They decided that they were signs telling about the downfall of the Aztec empire.

quezalcoatl.

(4)

One day in 1518, messengers came to the palace of Montezuma. They told him that strange ships had been seen off the eastern coast. Astronomers gave Montezuma an explanation for the ships: Quetzalcoatl was returning from the land of the rising sun. According to Aztec legend, Quetzalcoatl was a god— the giver of knowledge. About 500 years earlier, around the year 1000, the legend described how Quetzalcoatl had sailed into the ocean east of Mexico. He had promised to come back to Mexico and named 1519 as the year of his return.

The Fall of Tenochtitlan

In April 1519, the strange ships landed on the coast of Mexico. They carried 16 horses and 555 men. The leader was Hernando Cortez. Cortez had been sent by Spain to search for gold.

Montezuma sent ambassadors to greet Cortez and his men. They brought rich gifts of gold, jade, and silver. When Cortez saw all this wealth, he decided to conquer the Aztecs.

Cortez marched inland to Tenochtitlan. He put Montezuma in prison and made himself the ruler of Mexico. Some of the Indian tribes who hated the powerful Aztecs supported him.

Meeting of Montezuma and Cortez

UNITED STATES

GULF OF CALIFORNIA

PACIFIC OCEAN

MEXICO

GULF OF MEXICO

Cabo Catoche

Xalapa
Vera Cruz

Tlatlauqui

Tenochtitlan
Cuernavaca
Taxco
Tlaxcala
Tepoztlan

Campeche

CARIBBEAN SEA

———— Cortez' route

The Spanish then made a terrible mistake. While watching an Aztec religious ceremony, one officer thought the excited crowds were going to attack the Spanish. He ordered his men to fire cannons on the crowd. More than 3,000 people were killed.

A terrible war broke out. Some of the Indian tribes again sided with the Spanish. The Aztecs, however, fought for a long time and drove the Spaniards out of the city. But Cortez and his men finally conquered Tenochtitlan in 1521, wrecking it as they passed through.

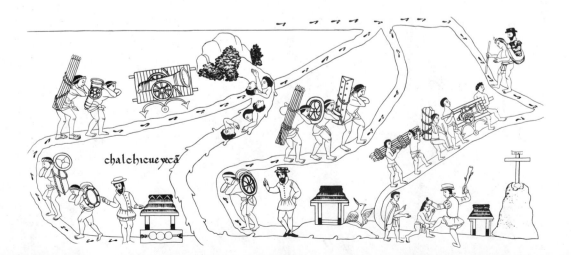

169

Copolco
Zoi nucca ỹ
capitan.

yeq̃tla ti tetzavitl
yn mal ques.

Tepoztlan Under the Spanish

Tepoztlan changed when the Aztecs conquered it. Now it changed again. The king of Spain rewarded Cortez for his victory by giving him several Indian villages. Tepoztlan was one of them. Tepoztlan now came under the government set up by the Spanish and had to pay taxes to it.

Tochtli was the great-grandson of Quauhtli. As he grew up, he saw the new things that the Spanish brought to Tepoztlan.

Cortez rewarded his Spanish soldiers by giving them power and land—the land of the Indians. New rulers and landowners came to Tepoztlan. They brought oxen and plows from Spain to help work the land. They brought horses and donkeys to ride and to carry things. They also brought pigs and chickens and cows and fruit trees to provide more food. They built large houses on big estates called haciendas. They built the wide plaza in the village. They made crisscrossing streets and paved some of the streets with stones. Tochtli grew up in a village that his great-grandfather would not have recognized.

The Spaniards did not do all of this work themselves. They made the Indians work for them. The Indians were forced to farm the landowners' fields, build roads and buildings, work as servants, and mine gold and silver with equipment brought from Spain. Tochtli and other Indians from Tepoztlan often had to work far from home. They might work in the mines at Taxco or on Cortez' hacienda in Cuernavaca.

Tochtli learned many new skills when the Spanish came. He learned how to guide a plow and how to take care of farm animals. He learned how to mine silver and gold. But these skills did not help him when he returned to his home. His field was too small and rocky for a plow, even if he could have afforded one. He had no farm animals and there was no gold or silver on his land.

The coming of the Spaniards also changed another important part of Tochtli's life: the gods he worshiped. His ancestors had prayed to Indian gods like Tepoztecatl. Tepoztecatl was the god who protected Tepoztlan. But the Spaniards brought a new religion. Catholic missionaries came to Tepoztlan.

Soon Tepoztlan had its own churches. Tochtli became a Catholic. He took part in the fiestas which celebrated religious holidays with colorful parades and masses at church.

INDEPENDENT MEXICO

Viva Mexico!

In 1810 a Mexican priest, Father Miguel Hidalgo, set off a revolution that would affect the lives of almost everyone in Mexico. Father Hidalgo was a Creole. That means he was of Spanish blood but was born in Mexico. Unlike many Creoles, he worked to help the Indians. In the poor, tiny town of Dolores, he helped the Indians plant grapes. The Spanish government had forbidden the growing of grapes in Mexico because it did not want Mexico competing with the Spanish grape industry. With money made from the grapes, Father Hidalgo helped the Indians start other industries. Finally, he decided to lead the Indians in a revolt against Spanish rule.

On September 16, 1810, he called the people of Dolores together. *"Viva Mexico!*—Long live Mexico!" he shouted. "Long live independence! Death to bad government!" The people took up Father Hidalgo's cry—the *Grito de Dolores*.

Father Hidalgo's rebel army was defeated. But he had started change. A series of revolutions followed, and by 1821 Mexico had won its independence from Spain.

Today, Father Hidalgo's cry is repeated every independence day. At midnight on September 16, the president of Mexico shouts the *Grito de Dolores* from the balcony of the national palace. The people echo his cry, *"Viva Mexico!"*

Mexico's president rides proudly into the capital city of his newly independent nation.

An Indian President

After Mexico gained its independence, the Creoles still kept their haciendas and the Indian peasants still worked on them. The Indians grew their own food on the community hillsides. They used tools like hoes and digging sticks. In Mexico City, the people in the new government were too busy struggling for power to worry about the Indians.

In 1857 Benito Juarez, Mexico's first Indian president, came to power. Juarez started a railroad. He built many schools. He put in a constitution that took some of the power away from the Creoles. But things in Tepoztlan remained much the same.

Mexico Modernizes

Toward the end of the nineteenth century, the United States, as well as many European countries, began to modernize rapidly. Mexico faced a new problem. To keep up with these countries and to trade with them, Mexico had to modernize, too. It had to have telephones and telegraphs so its business people could contact each other quickly. It had to get roads, railroads, and better seaports so goods could be moved to distant markets faster.

Putting up telephone poles, stringing wires, laying tracks, and building roads cost money. To get this money, Mexico needed people and countries with money to spare. These people and countries might lend money to Mexico in the hopes that they could make a profit. Mexico needed foreign investors since few Mexicans had money to spare.

CHANGE UNDER DIAZ

Porfirio Diaz became president of Mexico in 1876. He overthrew the government then in power. Except for the four years between 1880 and 1884, Diaz was president of Mexico until 1911.

President Diaz found many ways to attract investors—especially Americans—to Mexico. By jailing political opponents and stuffing ballot boxes with his own name during elections, he made sure he kept himself in office. Then investors could be sure that no revolutions would interrupt the long work of building railroads or roads. They would not have to worry about revolutions causing them to lose money.

Foreigners had also feared Mexico's famous bandits who robbed people traveling on the roads. Diaz started a special police force, the *rurales*. They knew how to deal with outlaws.

Finally, Diaz gave foreign investors many benefits. He sold Mexican land, oil fields, and gold and silver mines to them at bargain prices. In Tepoztlan, wealthy landowners sold much of Tepoztlan's community land to foreigners. By 1904, of the 10 million people in Mexico, 9½ million owned no land at all.

Under Diaz, Mexico began to modernize. Telephones were put in, roads were improved, and railroads were built. One railroad connected Tepoztlan with Cuernavaca and Mexico City. The railroad company hired villagers as railroad workers and paid them good wages. It also paid for the land it used. The Tepoztecans used this money to pipe water into the village, to build a park, and to light the streets with oil lamps.

CHANGE AFTER THE REVOLUTION

In 1910 revolution swept Mexico. Diaz, who was getting very old, had promised to call an election so a new president could be chosen. But as the election drew near, Diaz decided that he would continue to rule. Political leaders who hoped to succeed Diaz revolted. Francisco Madero—one of the leaders—promised to give the peasants land if they supported him. Many peasants joined the revolt. Pedro Martinez, the peasant interviewed by Oscar Lewis, joined the forces led by Emiliano Zapata. Zapata, a peasant himself, was a follower of Madero. But when Madero failed to give the peasants land, Zapata refused to support him.

In 1917 a new constitution was adopted. Slowly, the aims of the revolution were being won. Ownership of land by foreigners was to be ended. And a new government started turning community lands back to the Indians.

Emiliano Zapata

Orozco, Jose Clemente, *Zapatistas*, 1931. Oil on canvas,
45″ x 55″. Collection, The Museum of Modern Art, New
York

Zapatistas

    New technology came to Tepoztlan. Corn mills
were built, so the people did not have to spend so
much time grinding corn by hand. With time to
spare, people began to grow fruit and to raise animals
for sale at market. Sewing machines helped to clothe
people better, too. A new road connected Tepoztlan
with the Mexico City-Cuernavaca highway. Two bus
lines started, owned jointly by the villagers. New
schools were also built for the village children.

Some Ways To Study Change

EDUCATION IN TEPOZTLAN

Squadron 201 is the name of a school built in Tepoztlan following World War II. It was named after a squadron of Mexican aviators who fought in the Philippines during the war. When the squadron returned to Mexico, the president of Mexico asked each member of the squadron to name something he wanted. Most asked for money for their families. But not Angel Bocanegra. He wanted a school for his village, Tepoztlan.

Nonmodern people expect their children to live in a world just like theirs. They prepare the children for this world by taking them with them wherever they go. They teach them to do the things they do.

Modern people know that their children's world will be different from theirs. The modern world changes so fast that no one can know what the future will be like. Modern children go to school to learn the skills they will need to live in a world they do not yet know.

The number of children who go to school is a measure of modernization. In the six years that Dr. Lewis studied Tepoztlan, the number of elementary school students increased from 750 to 900. In the same six years, the number of high school students increased from 54 to 110.

School children in Tepoztlan learn the same basic skills you learn in school: reading, writing, mathematics, and good citizenship. Each year some of the high school graduates go to the university in Mexico City.

Now, some years after Dr. Lewis studied the
schools in Tepoztlan, attendance is still growing.
More and more, students are attending high school
and the higher elementary grades. More and more,
parents in Tepoztlan want their children to learn the
skills taught in school.

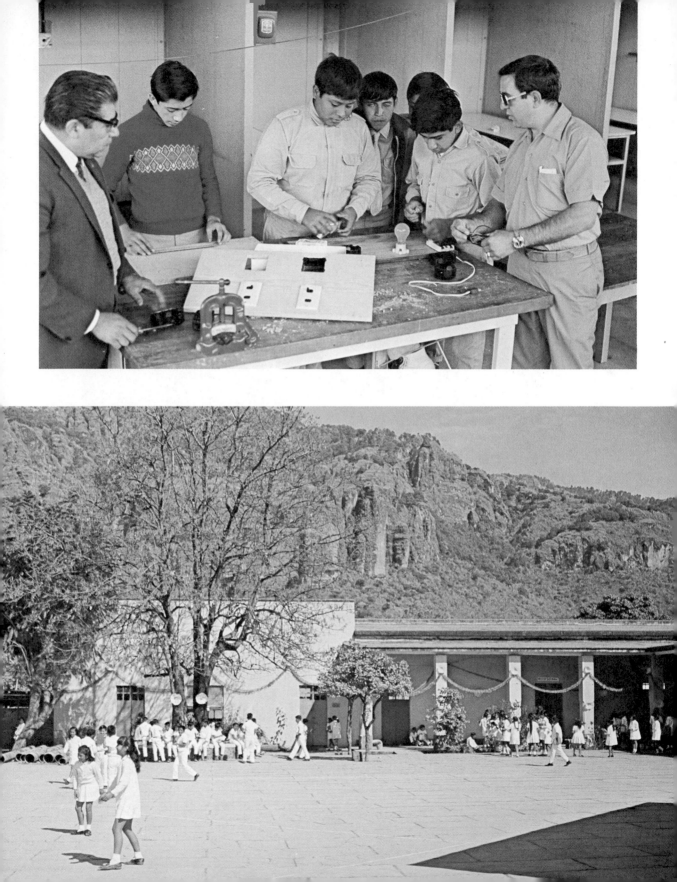

THE MARTINEZ CHILDREN GROW UP

Between 1943 and 1963, Oscar Lewis went to Tepoztlan a number of times. He interviewed the Martinez family and kept track of what was happening to them. He was interested in how their lives changed over a period of time.

Having seen the Martinez children grow up, Dr. Lewis was especially interested in them. Did their lives differ from those of their parents? Did the lives of the older children differ from those of the younger ones? By looking for answers to these questions, an anthropologist can get clues about how modernization affects people's lives. Dr. Lewis learned the following information about the Martinez children.

Felipe was not a healthy child. When he was about 11 years old, he lost an eye in an accident. He quit school shortly after that.

Felipe went to work on the community land that his father farmed. But he and his father fought. Felipe left home a number of times but always returned. After the death of his mother, he left home for good and went to Mexico City. There he worked as a fruit-juice seller and night watchman.

Felipe

Mexico City

Mexico City

Martin left school when he was 12. He had finished three grades.

Martin worked first for his father and then as a farmhand on a neighboring hacienda. Between planting seasons, he worked in a bakery to learn to be a baker. When he was 21, he went to Mexico City and worked there as a baker for eight months. When his mother became ill, Martin came home. He went to work as a farm laborer. Like his brothers, he gave most of his wages to his father.

After working seven years as a farm laborer, Martin got a job as a master baker. He still lived with his father and helped with the family expenses. Sometimes he worked in the fields. When he was 36, Martin married. He hopes to buy a baker's oven and to set up his own business.

Martin

Ricardo went to school for three years. When he was about to enter the fourth grade, his father took him out of school. He was 15 years old. He went to work but did not like being ordered around by his brothers. When he was 23, he left home.

Ricardo joined the navy in 1955. He worked in the kitchen and in the tailor's shop. When he left the navy, he found work as a kitchen helper in a city north of Tepoztlan.

Ricardo is now married and has a steady job as a cook's helper. He saves some money and sends money to his father or to one of his brothers. He and his wife visit his family in Tepoztlan every year.

Ricardo

Machrina

When Machrina was 16 years old, her parents took her out of school. They wanted her to stay at home so she could grind the corn, cook the meals, and wash and iron the clothes. Machrina liked school and wanted to become a dressmaker. But she did what her parents asked her to do. Shortly after her twentieth birthday, Machrina married.

Machrina's husband treated her badly, so she came back home. She and her child lived with her father and brothers. She did the washing, ironing, grinding, and cooking. Her father and brothers rarely gave her any money. Machrina said that made her sad.

When Machrina was 34 she remarried. Her new husband worked for a bus line. For a short time they lived in her father's house, then they moved to a house of their own.

Moises entered school when he was six. He finished six grades and then went on to the village secondary school. Moises enjoyed school. He had many friends and was able to go swimming every day. He learned to dance and even went on school trips.

Moises graduated and then entered the state university in Cuernavaca. With his brothers' help, he finished school and became a teacher.

Like his brothers, Moises visits his family regularly. Two years after his mother's death, he bought adobe, roof tiles, and other building materials so he could build another house for his family.

Moises

German

German is Pedro's grandson. He was raised by his grandparents. He did not enter school until he was 8 years old but, urged on by Pedro, Machrina, and Moises, he stayed in school. He finished secondary school and then went on to college. He, too, became a teacher.

IS TEPOZTLAN MODERN?

You have seen that anthropologists study change and that villages change by becoming modern. How has Tepoztlan changed? Do you think it is modern or nonmodern?

6

World Markets

The Cocoa Bean Market

RAIN IN GHANA

It was 3:05 A.M. A telephone rang in Hershey, Pennsylvania. A man turned over in his bed and picked up the telephone. The voice at

the other end of the wire was tense. "Heavy rains are reported in Ghana," the voice said. The man from Hershey put down the telephone. He lay awake worrying the rest of the night.

COCOA BEAN PRODUCERS AND USERS

Ghana is the world's largest producer of cocoa beans. It grows about two-fifths of all the cocoa beans. Nigeria is next. It grows about one-fifth of the world's cocoa beans. Brazil ranks third. It grows about one-tenth of the world's cocoa beans.

Cocoa beans are used to make chocolate. The United States is the world's largest user of cocoa beans. American companies buy almost one-fifth of all the cocoa beans grown. West Germany is the second largest user of cocoa beans.

In the United States, the Hershey Foods Corporation is among the biggest buyers of cocoa beans. Can you guess why the man in Hershey, Pennsylvania, cares about the weather in Ghana? Do you think that two places so far from each other could have been linked together like this during the days of Shang China?

Moulding chocolate bars

BUYING AND SELLING COCOA BEANS

An International Market

Cocoa beans are bought and sold differently from the way goods are bought and sold at Tepoztlan's market. Cocoa beans are bought and sold on an international market. This market is not a particular place like Tepoztlan's market. The international cocoa bean market is a term used to describe the buying and selling of cocoa beans by people all over the world.

Most of the buying and selling of cocoa beans is done at places called exchanges. A cocoa exchange is a place where buyers and sellers meet to agree on a price for a certain amount of cocoa beans. There are cocoa exchanges in New York, Chicago, London, Paris, and Amsterdam. The New York Cocoa Exchange is the biggest.

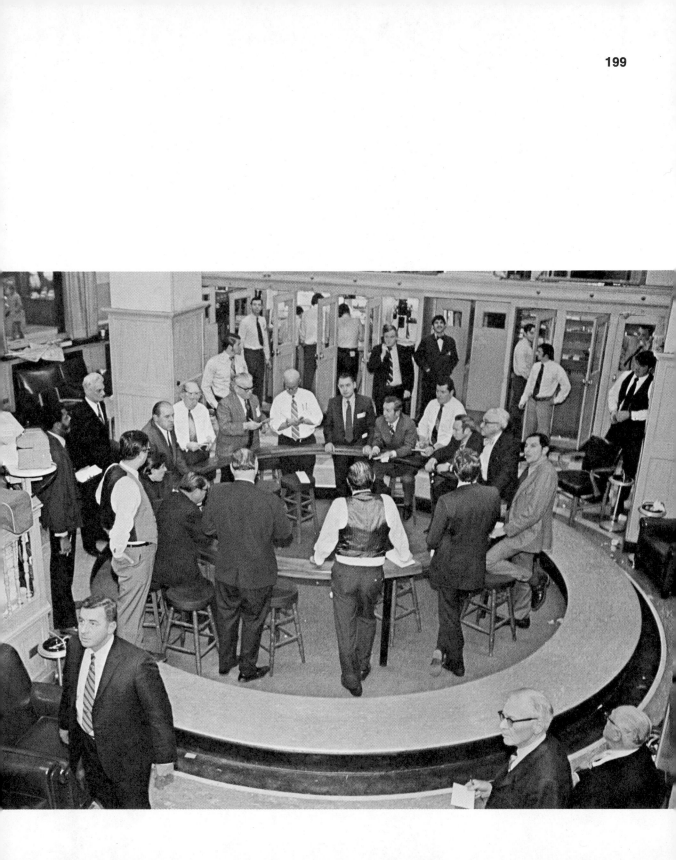

The buying and selling of cocoa beans differs in another important way from the buying and selling of goods in Tepoztlan. The farmer who grows the cocoa beans and the chocolate manufacturer who will buy them generally do not come to the exchange. Sellers usually hire a broker who sells their cocoa beans for them at the highest possible price. The buyers generally carry on their business through a broker, too. The broker tries to buy cocoa beans for the buyer at the lowest possible price.

The cocoa beans are not brought to the exchange either. The buying and selling of cocoa beans takes place on paper. Farmers sell their crops even before they are planted. When buyers purchase a crop, they get a futures contract. The contract states that a person has purchased a certain amount of cocoa beans to be delivered at some future date.

A Sale

A sale is started when, for example, a farmer tells a broker to sell futures contracts for the next July for 30,000 pounds. This means that the farmer expects to harvest 30,000 pounds of cocoa beans and to deliver them the following July. The broker puts the contracts up for sale at the New York Cocoa Exchange.

At the same time, the Hershey Foods Corporation begins to make plans. Company planners decide to order 30,000 pounds of cocoa beans for July. The company buyer telephones Hershey's broker in New York. "Buy one July futures contract for 30,000 pounds of cocoa beans," the buyer says.

Wrapping and packaging chocolate bars

The broker telephones the person they have
stationed on the floor of the New York Cocoa
Exchange. This person is called a floor broker. The
broker says, "Buy one July at the market." The floor
broker leaves the telephone booth and enters a ring
in the center of the floor. All buying and selling of
cocoa beans at the New York Cocoa Exchange takes
place in this ring. Many floor brokers stand in the
ring, shouting the prices of contracts they want to
buy or sell.

Standing in the ring, the floor broker yells,
"25 for July." Hershey's broker is offering to pay 25
cents for each pound of cocoa beans they buy and

is saying that they want them next July. Another floor broker shouts, "July at 25½." This broker is selling a contract for cocoa beans to be delivered the following July. The price is 25½ cents for each pound of cocoa beans. The floor broker for Hershey thinks that 25½ cents is a good price. Hershey's broker places the order by turning to the floor broker selling the contract and saying, "I'll take it."

The floor broker for Hershey calls back to the brokerage firm with news of the purchase. The firm telephones Hershey. At the same time, this sale and all other sales, even those made in Chicago and at the cocoa exchanges in Europe, are recorded on a large chalkboard. Reports of cocoa bean sales are published daily and are telegraphed over the cocoa exchange ticker system. A ticker is a type of

telegraph that automatically prints things like prices on a paper ribbon. The paper ribbon is called a ticker tape. Ticker tapes are watched by cocoa bean growers, chocolate producers, and brokers all over the world. They want to know the amount of cocoa beans being bought and sold and how much is being paid for them.

In July the Hershey Foods Corporation will be notified that 30,000 pounds of cocoa beans have been delivered to its warehouse. Since Hershey agreed to pay $25\frac{1}{2}$ cents for each pound of cocoa beans, it has to pay the cocoa bean grower $7,650.00.

Chocolate kisses emerging from cooling tunnels

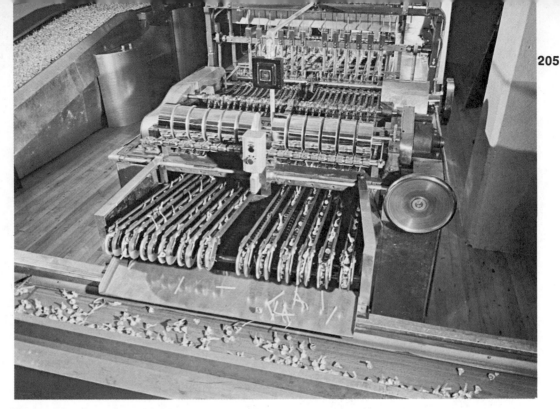

Wrapping chocolate kisses

Price

Hershey paid 25½ cents for each pound of cocoa beans. Cocoa beans have sold for as little as 4 cents for each pound and as much as 72 cents for each pound. What determines price?

Price depends on supply and demand. The supply of cocoa beans refers to the number of tons of cocoa beans produced all over the world each year. Demand for cocoa beans is created by the people who want to buy cocoa beans.

Anything that affects supply and demand can affect price. Can you figure out why? What if the crop of cocoa beans is large, but chocolate producers in America decide to stop making candy bars? How will this decision affect the demand for cocoa beans? How will it affect the price of cocoa beans?

A WORLD SYSTEM

Now do you know why the man in Hershey, Pennsylvania, cares about the weather in Ghana? Politics in Africa, sugar crop diseases in South America, dockworkers' strikes in Europe, and a rise in the price of milk in the United States can all affect the international cocoa bean market. They can affect cocoa bean growers in Ghana and chocolate producers in the United States. They can even affect you and the price of your chocolate bar.

Sorting chocolate kisses for packaging

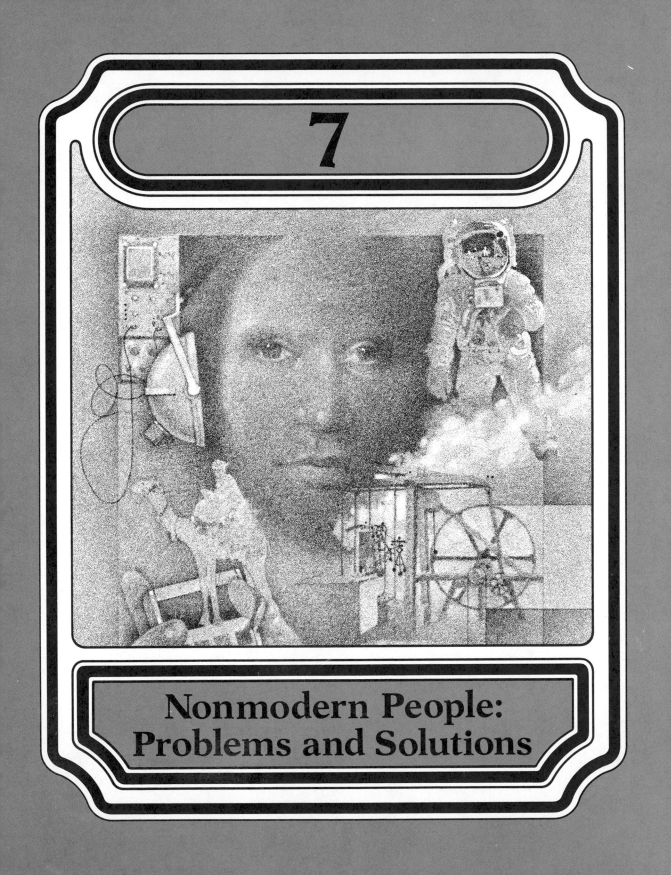

7

Nonmodern People: Problems and Solutions

Standard of Living in India

In 1970 there were 3.6 billion people in the world. Of these people, 552 million, or about 15 out of every 100, lived in India.

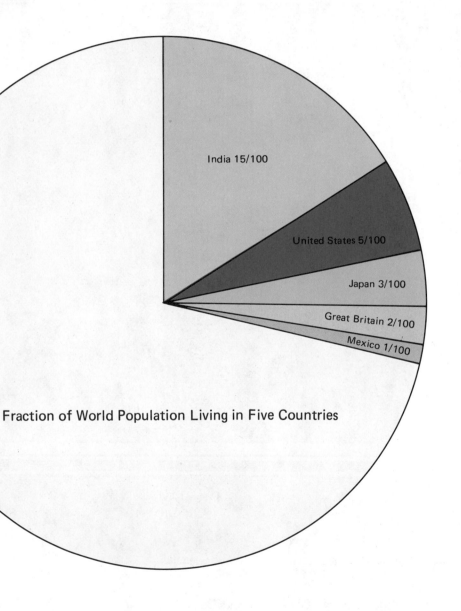

India 15/100

United States 5/100

Japan 3/100

Great Britain 2/100

Mexico 1/100

Fraction of World Population Living in Five Countries

VILLAGE INDIA

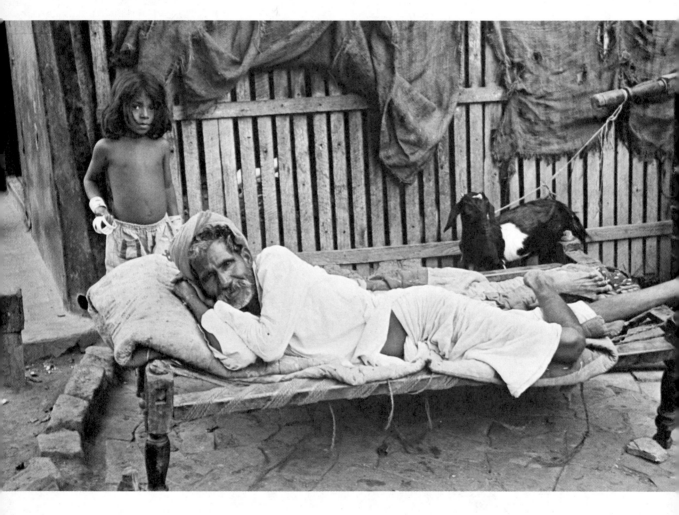

ECONOMISTS MEASURE STANDARD OF LIVING

India's many people face many problems. Economists describe some of these problems by saying that India's people have a low standard of living. As anthropologists study and measure material culture, economists study and measure standard of living. Here is one tool economists use to measure standard of living:

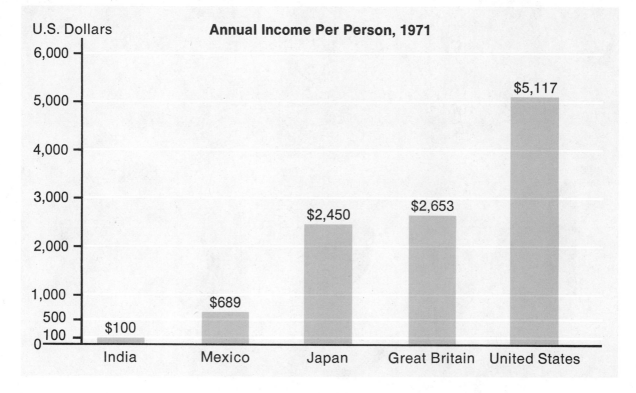

Annual Income Per Person, 1971

U.S. Dollars

India	Mexico	Japan	Great Britain	United States
$100	$689	$2,450	$2,653	$5,117

NEW GOALS

In 1947 India became an independent nation.
It was no longer under British rule. This new
India set new goals for itself. One of them was to
raise its standard of living.

Where Do You Start?

When India decided to raise its standard of living, its first problem was where to start. Most of the people of India have few possessions: simple clothes, a few copper or earthenware pots, a cot to sleep on, and a kerosene lamp to see by at night. They have no electricity, no running water. They cannot read or write. And they have less food than they need to stay healthy. Most of their diet is rice. When people have so little, where do you start to improve their standard of living?

ASKING THE ECONOMISTS

Economists can help countries make decisions like this one. Economists understand that India, like all the countries in the world, has limited resources. They know that India cannot do everything at once. If resources are used for one purpose, they are not available for other purposes. So economists study what might happen if resources are used for one purpose rather than another. Their studies can help people make choices. India's leaders asked some economists to help them decide where they should start to raise the standard of living.

The first group of economists said that one reason for India's low standard of living was its large population. They recommended that India educate its people to have smaller families.

The second group said that India's standard of living would continue to be low until India had more industries to employ more people and produce more goods. They recommended that India build steel plants and plants for generating electricity.

The third group of economists said that India's standard of living was low mainly because the land had been divided into very small plots. These small plots were unsuitable for modern farming methods. They recommended that India reorganize the land into more efficient units.

The fourth group said that India's standard of living was low because its people could not trade with each other. Especially in rural areas, it is difficult to transport goods from one area to another. These economists recommended that India build roads to link the people together.

The fifth group of economists said that India's standard of living was low because the methods used to plant and harvest crops were poor and because India's soil needed fertilizing. The land had been used for too many years without adding fertilizers to renew the soil. The amount of food produced by each acre of land in India was very small. These economists recommended that India increase the productivity of each acre of land.

The economists agreed that, ideally, India should do all of these things at once. But India could not afford to do everything at once. Its resources were limited. India's leaders had to decide where to start. They studied information gathered about their country to help them make their decision.

ECONOMISTS BUILD THEIR CASE

Each group of economists used data to support their recommendations to India's leaders. This is how one group of economists, the fifth group, supported their recommendation that India use its resources to increase the harvest on each acre of land:

Pounds of Rice Grown on Each Hectare* of Land, 1963

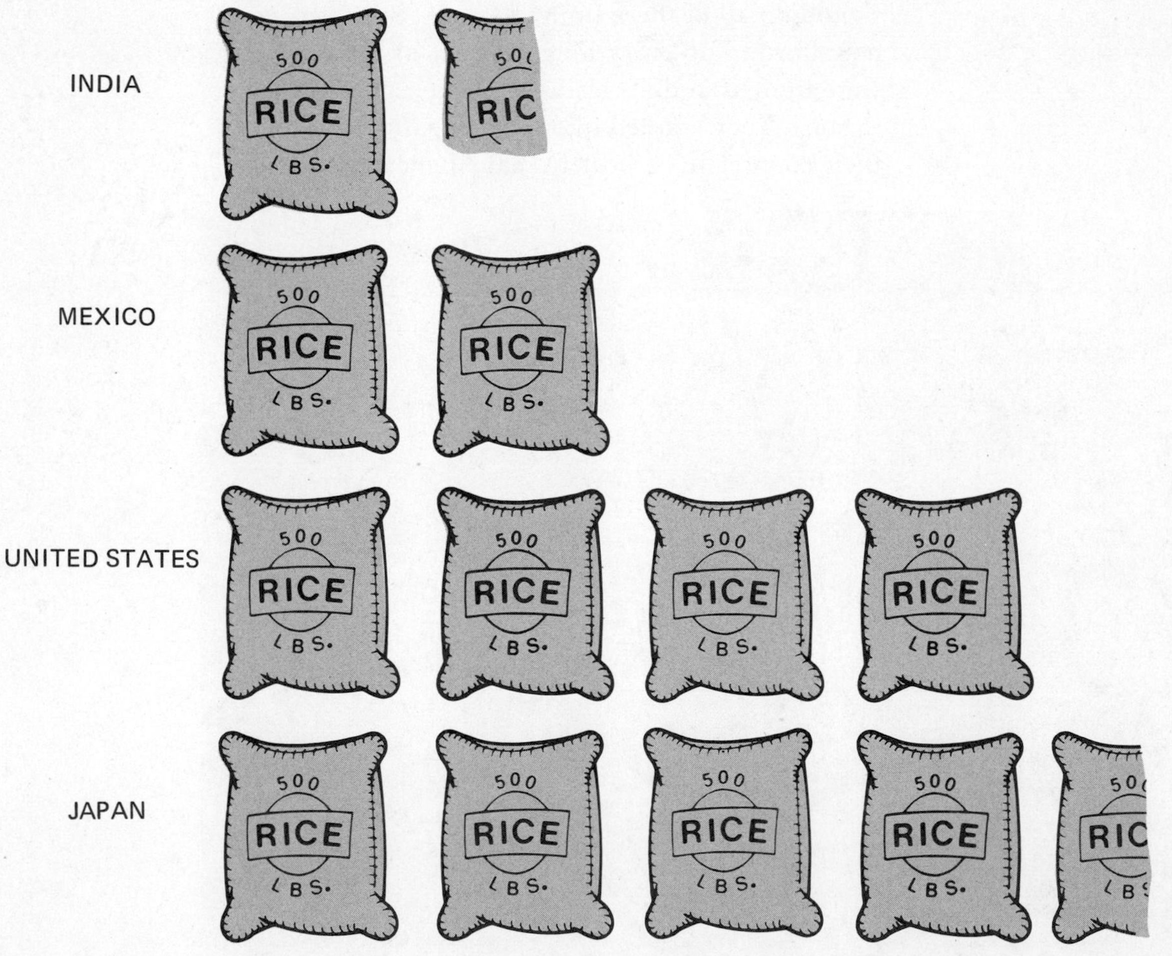

INDIA

MEXICO

UNITED STATES

JAPAN

*1 hectare = 2½ acres

This group also decided to collect information to show India's leaders how much food grain was actually being produced in India. Here is what they discovered:

Food Grain Production in India

Year	Food Grain Produced (in millions of metric tons)
1960	84
1961	85
1962	85
1963	89
1964	93
1965	80
1966	80

Was India producing more or less grain every year?

A table, like the one above, is one way to present these statistics. Here is another way:

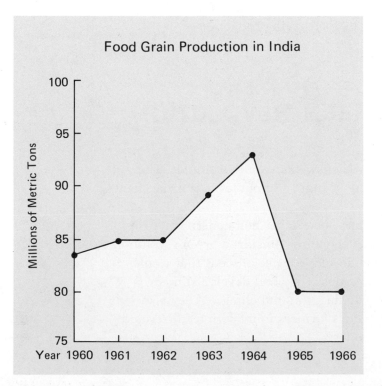

Line graphs, like the one on page 219, are often used by economists. They show change more clearly than numbers in a table.

The economists from the fifth group knew that they still did not have enough data to convince India's leaders to put more of India's resources into increasing food production. So they also included the following information:

Population of India

Year	Population (in millions of people)
1960	429
1961	436
1962	450
1963	464
1964	475
1965	487
1966	499

Which was going up more steadily—India's population or its food grain production?

THE GREEN REVOLUTION

India's leaders made up their minds. They would use more of India's resources to improve food production.

India and some other nonmodern countries decided to use technology to start a green revolution. Scientists had developed special seeds that would produce more crops. They had developed them especially for India's soil and climate. They also introduced India's farmers to modern fertilizer and farming machinery.

Here is how the government's new efforts to improve food production worked in one part of India—Tanjore. The director of the new plan in Tanjore was Mooliyil Mukundan. He recruited 750 workers from the villages in Tanjore. He showed them a new kind of rice seed developed by Indian scientists especially for India's soil and climate. The new seed did not need as much fertilizer as other seeds. And since it grew faster than the old

seed, farmers could grow two rice crops in the time it used to take to grow one. Scientists felt that this new seed would raise rice production—if only the farmers could be persuaded to try it.

Mukundan and his assistants spread out into the villages of Tanjore. They showed farmers the new seed and how to grow it. More than 200,000 farmers in Tanjore learned about the seed and agreed to try it. In 1967, with the help of good monsoon rains, Tanjore's farmers grew 450,000 tons more rice than they had the season before.

All over India, men like Mukundan worked with scientists and farmers to improve food grain production. This was the result:

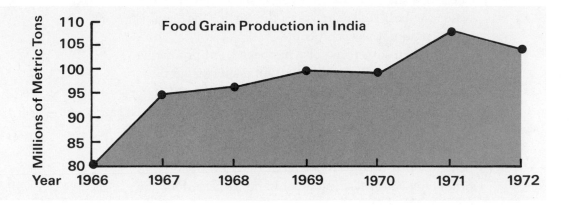

Did the green revolution improve the life of India's villagers?

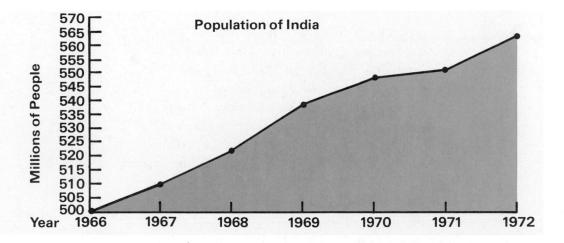

Where Is the Green Revolution Going?

In 1970 and 1971 the green revolution continued to work. But in 1972 things were different. The monsoon rains failed to come that year. Without water the best seeds shrivel in the earth. Once again India could not feed its people.

Then something else happened. Oil producing countries raised the price of oil. In a short time the price of oil doubled and then doubled again. Oil is used to produce fertilizer. The new seeds produced to make the green revolution need fertilizer to do their best. India had very little oil of its own. It had to buy the oil it used to make fertilizer from the oil producing countries. India could no longer afford the fertilizer it needed to keep its fields green.

The green revolution seemed to be ending for India before it really had a chance to get started.

A World Food Crisis

To make matters worse, the United States, the world's largest food producer and exporter, was having problems. The United States had used technology and cheap energy to produce crop surpluses. But now, energy was no longer cheap. Most Americans still ate well—nearly a ton of grain per person a year. But food prices went up and up. Most Americans were not happy about sending surplus grain out of the country. This would push high American prices still higher.

Is there a solution to the world food problem? Some people want to remove salt from sea water so desert land can be irrigated and made productive. This would take a lot of energy and energy is expensive now. Others think that some way must be found to keep the world's population from growing so fast. What do you think?

8

Modern People:
Problems and Solutions

Defining Poverty in America

Most of India's people are poor. One reason is that India does not grow enough food for all of its people. Modern technology can help India solve its poverty problem.

American technology grows more food than Americans eat. Yet many Americans are still poor. The causes of poverty in the United States are different from those in India.

For the next few weeks, you are going to investigate the problem of poverty in the United States. You will try, first, to define the problem: What is American poverty? One way to define something is to say what it is *not*. Compare the United States with India and you can say what American poverty is not. For example, poverty in the United States is not growing too little wheat because of dry land and simple tools. It is not a lack of industries to create jobs and to produce goods. These are some of the many things poverty in America is not. Can you think of at least one thing that poverty in America is?

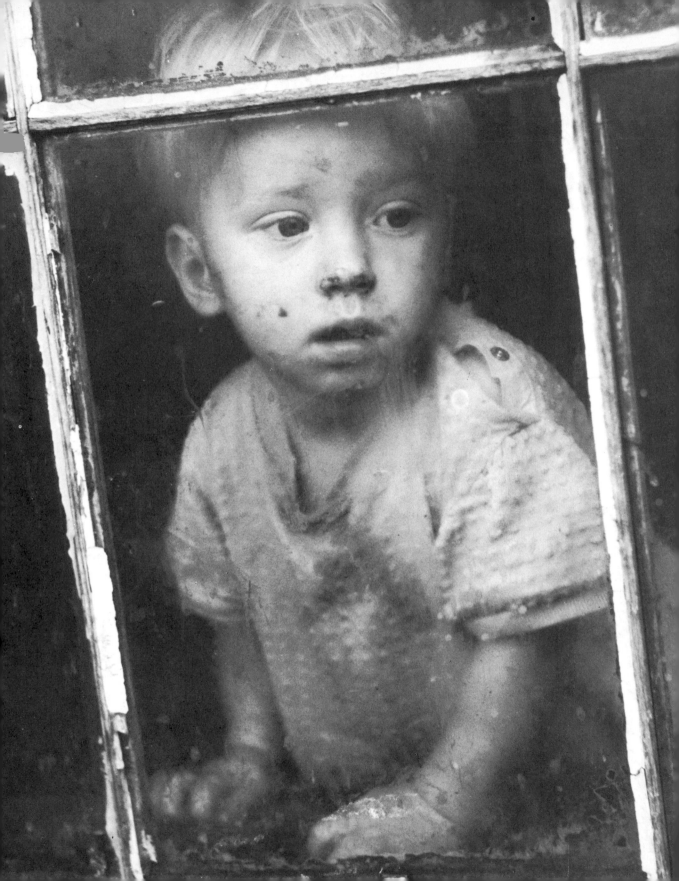

THE PRESIDENT WANTS A DEFINITION

In 1963 the President of the United States started thinking about this very same question: What is poverty in America? He wanted to ask Congress to do something about it. But he couldn't know what action to ask for until he found out what the problem was. So he went to his economic advisers and asked them for the answers to these questions: What is poverty in the United States? How many poor people are there in America? What can the nation do to help them and how much might it cost?

Collecting Information

The Census Bureau is a government office that collects statistics. It was set up to collect population statistics every ten years, so that each state would know how many representatives it could send to the United States Congress. But government leaders often needed other kinds of statistics to help them solve problems. They asked the Census Bureau to collect those statistics, too.

In the 1930's, the nation's biggest problem was poverty. In 1933 one-fourth of the labor force was out of work. Those who were working earned less than usual. Stores could not sell their goods. Many Americans were poor.

A painting of an employment agency in the 1930's

Isaac Soyer, *Employment Agency*. Oil on canvas, 34¼" x 45". 1937. Collection Whitney Museum of American Art, New York

When the time came for the census of 1940, Congress told the Census Bureau to collect statistics about the poor. The census takers went around the country, asking people questions about their income. They repeated the questions in 1950, 1960, and 1970.

In 1963 the President's economic advisers looked at the census data for 1960. They wanted to figure out the average income for American families. First they added up the yearly incomes of American families who had reported their income. Then they divided the total family income by the number of families reporting. They found that the average income for American families was $6,000 a year.

Making Categories

Just knowing the average income of American families did not help the President's economic advisers to answer the President's questions. They needed more data.

Most census information comes into the Census Bureau on forms mailed to families or filled out by the census takers. Economists take the information on those forms and put it into categories. By doing this, they can find answers to questions.

The categories they use depend upon the questions they want to answer. Here are some of the categories into which income information from the census can be divided. What questions does each category answer?

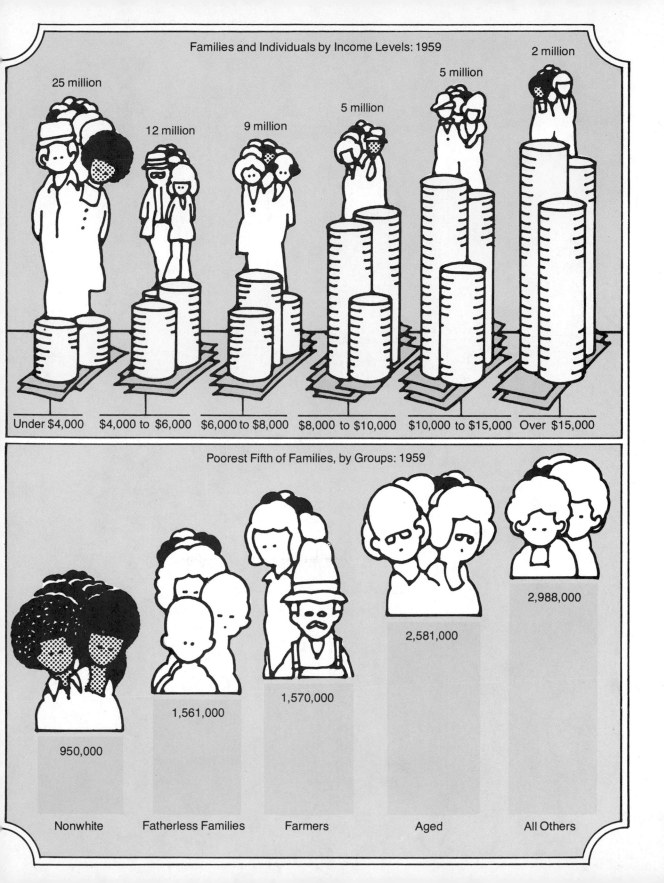

Families and Individuals by Income Levels: 1959

25 million — Under $4,000
12 million — $4,000 to $6,000
9 million — $6,000 to $8,000
5 million — $8,000 to $10,000
5 million — $10,000 to $15,000
2 million — Over $15,000

Poorest Fifth of Families, by Groups: 1959

Nonwhite — 950,000
Fatherless Families — 1,561,000
Farmers — 1,570,000
Aged — 2,581,000
All Others — 2,988,000

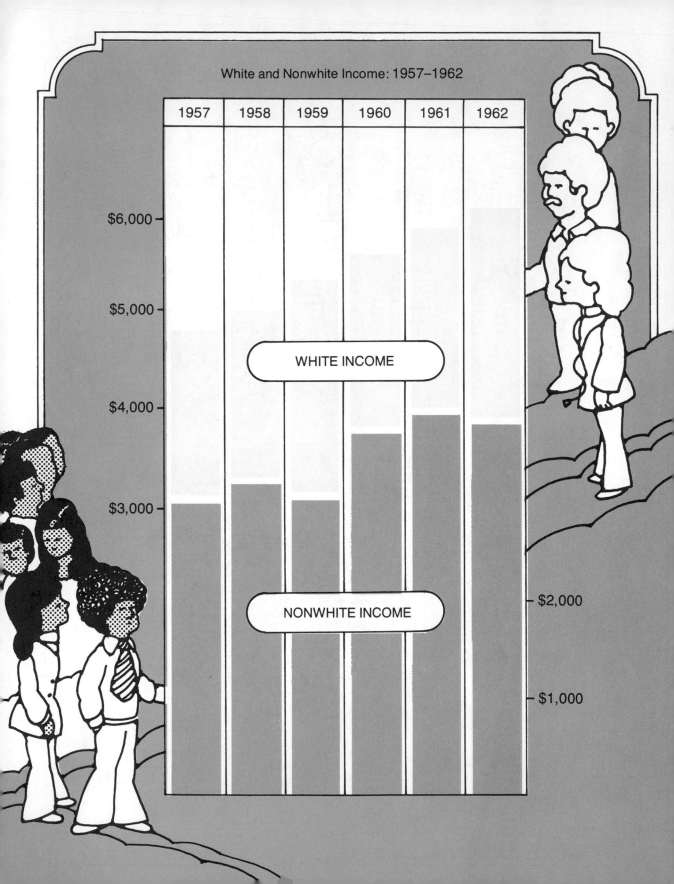

White and Nonwhite Income: 1957–1962

| 1957 | 1958 | 1959 | 1960 | 1961 | 1962 |

$6,000

$5,000

WHITE INCOME

$4,000

$3,000

NONWHITE INCOME

$2,000

$1,000

233

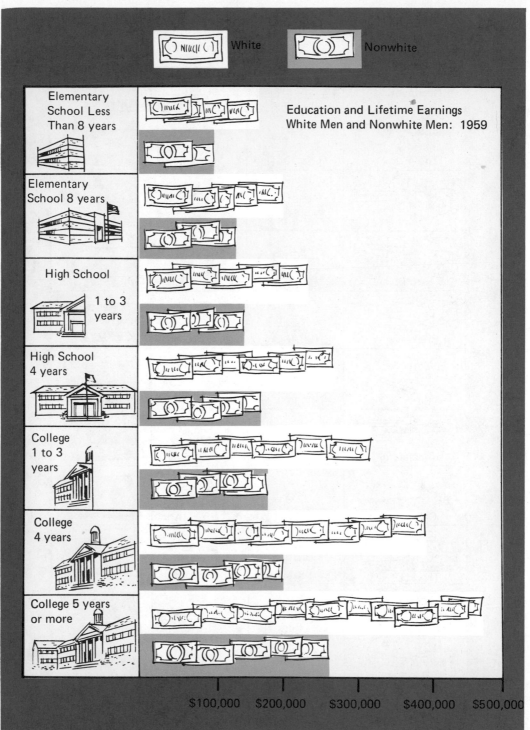

Education and Lifetime Earnings
White Men and Nonwhite Men: 1959

White	Nonwhite

Elementary School Less Than 8 years

Elementary School 8 years

High School 1 to 3 years

High School 4 years

College 1 to 3 years

College 4 years

College 5 years or more

$100,000 $200,000 $300,000 $400,000 $500,000

Occupation	Elementary School Graduates	High School Graduates	$ Difference
Toolmakers	$6,700	$7,300	$600
Plumbers	$5,700	$6,700	$1,000
Electricians	$6,100	$6,600	$500
Bricklayers	$5,100	$6,300	$1,200
Firemen	$5,300	$6,100	$800
Mechanics	$5,000	$5,900	$900
Carpenters	$4,800	$5,700	$900
Truck Drivers	$5,200	$5,700	$500
Bus Drivers	$4,400	$5,400	$1,000
Painters	$4,400	$5,100	$700

Education, Occupation and Income of
White Men: 1959

THE ECONOMIC ADVISERS DEFINE POVERTY

After the President's economic advisers categorized and studied the census data, they knew how many American families had incomes under $4,000. They knew the average income for families in America was $6,000. They knew how much a white man with an eighth-grade education could expect to earn, and how much a nonwhite man with the same education could expect to earn. But they still did not know exactly what poverty was or how to define it.

The President had asked his advisers to come up with a definition of poverty that would tell him how many Americans were poor. He realized that the definition would not be perfect. It would include some Americans who were not poor and leave out some who were poor. But he knew that when he asked Congress to do something about poverty, he had to be able to tell them about how many poor people there were in America.

The President's economic advisers went back
to their figures. They knew that some families
could live on less than others. Families living on
farms do not need as much money for food as
families living in New York City. They knew that
families with eight children need more money
than families with no children. And families living
in Maine need more money to keep warm in
the winter than families living in Mississippi.

Finally they made a decision. They would tell the President that any family of two or more with an income of less than $3,000 a year should be counted as poor. Single people with incomes under $1,500 a year should also be counted as poor. Their definition of poverty was far from perfect, and they knew it, but it was a start.

Anthropologists Study Poverty

Economists are not the only scientists who study the problem of poverty. Anthropologists are interested in poverty, too. Oscar Lewis, the anthropologist who studied Tepoztlan, also examined the problem of poverty. Dr. Lewis knew the statistics collected by the Census Bureau, but he was more interested in the daily lives of poor people.

Dr. Lewis had a theory that poverty is a way of living passed on from one generation to the next. To check his theory, he collected data by interviewing the poor. He listened closely to what they said and took photographs of the way they lived. He studied these words and pictures, looking for clues to the patterns of poverty.

For the next several days, you too will observe the poor. You will read a description of a poor family's home, and you will see the poor in pictures. You will study their words. Using this data, you will investigate Dr. Lewis' theory that poverty is a way of living passed on from one generation to the next.

DESCRIBING THE SETTING OF THE POOR

Dr. Lewis wrote about the poor in a book about a Puerto Rican family. In it he described their home in New York City. Part of the description follows:

Although the kitchen was clean and cheerful-looking, there were several cockroaches crawling on the walls and over the sink. On one side of the crowded room was a china cabinet, a large four-burner gas stove, and a table and three chairs. On the outer wall a combination sink and washtub was almost blocked by the refrigerator, making the washtub hard to get to. The kitchen walls had just been painted a bright green. They were decorated with religious calendars, plastic flowers, a fancy match holder, a plaster plaque of brightly colored fruit, and a new set of aluminum pans. Fresh red-and-white curtains hung at the window. The linoleum, although worn, was scrubbed clean. On a shelf above the kitchen door stood a homemade altar.

STUDYING THE WORDS OF THE POOR

Words Spoken by the Poor

Hugh McCaslin is the imaginary name of a person who lives in West Virginia. West Virginia is part of Appalachia. Appalachia refers to a group of states that include or border on the Appalachian Mountains.

Appalachia

Great natural beauty surrounds the people
of Appalachia.

So does great poverty.

Coal mines tunnel through the earth in Appalachia. Hugh McCaslin used to work in one of them. He was a powerful man until he was hurt. He was working in the mine when some earth caved in. Hugh's back was injured. He has not worked since. Hugh's doctor says he could do light work, like clerking in a bank or a legal office. But there aren't any banks or legal offices in the town where Hugh lives.

Hugh says it doesn't matter that he can't work in the mines. Most of the men he worked with who are strong and healthy don't have jobs either. Machines do their jobs now.

The McCaslins get a small pension because of Hugh's accident in the mine. But it is not enough to feed Hugh, his wife, and their children. Hugh's brother helps, and his four sisters help out, too. But Hugh says, "My daddy can't help except to sympathize and tell me it's a good thing I didn't get killed in that landslide and can see my boys grow up."

Here is what Hugh McCaslin has to say about himself:

I'll tell you, a man like me has a lot of time to think. I sit around here, day upon day, and what else do I have to keep my mind on but my thoughts? I can't work, and even if I could, there's no work to do, not around here, no sir.

My daddy, he was born right up the road in this here hollow, and his daddy, and back to a long time ago. There isn't anyone around here we're not kin to somehow, near or far.

I need some hope and it's in my kids, in their young age and the future they have, if they only get out of here before it's too late. Oh, I like it here. It's pretty, and all that. It's peaceful. I'm proud of us people. We've been here a long time, and we needed real guts to stay and last. And who wants to live in a big city? I've been in some of our cities, here in West Virginia, and they're no big value, from what I can see, not so far as bringing up a family. You have no land, no privacy, a lot of noise, and all that. But if it's between living and dying, I'll take living. And right here, right now, I think we're dying—dying away, slow but sure, every year more and more so.

Words Written
by the Poor

Claude Brown grew up in Harlem, a largely black community in New York City. He was one of the 950,000 nonwhites counted as poor in the 1960 census.

Claude spent about five years in reform schools. He eventually went to night school and graduated from high school in New York. He then went on to college. While there, he wrote a book about his experiences as a boy growing up in Harlem. The book is called *Manchild in the Promised Land*. The following story is part of it.

It was pretty cold; there was a lot of snow in the street. Traffic was moving at a snail's pace, almost at a standstill. Mama was complaining about the cold.

"Mama, why don't you complain to the landlord about this?"

A street in Harlem

"I called the office of the renting agency twice,
and they said he wasn't in. When I called the third
time, I spoke to him, but he said that it wasn't any
of his problem, and I'd have to fix it up myself.
I ain't got no money to be gettin' these windows
relined."

"Mama, I know better than that. Why don't you go up
to the housing commission and complain about it?"

"I ain't got no time to be goin' no place complainin'
about nothin'. I got all this housework to do, and
all this cookin'."

"Look, Mama, let's you and me go up there right
now. I'm gonna write out a complaint, and I want you
to sign it."

"I got all this washin' to do."

"Mama, you go on and you wash. I'm gon wait for
you; I'm gon help you wash."

Mama started washing the clothes. As soon as she finished that, she had to put the pot on the stove. Then she had to fix some lunch. As soon as she finished one thing, she would find another thing that she had to do right away. She just kept stalling for time.

Finally, after waiting for about three hours, when she couldn't find anything else to do, I said, "Look, Mama, come on, let's you and me go out there."

We went over to 145th Street. We were going to take the crosstown bus to Broadway, to the temporary housing-commission office.

We were waiting there. Because of the snowstorm, the buses weren't running well, so we waited there for a long time. Mama said, "Look, we'd better wait and go some other time."

I knew she wanted to get out of this, and I knew if I let her go and put it off to another time, it would never be done. I said, "Mama, we can take a cab."

"You got any money?"

"No."

"I ain't got none either. So we better wait until another time."

"Look, Mama, you wait right here on the corner. I'm going across the street to the pawnshop, and when I get back, we'll take a cab."

She waited there on the corner, and I went over to the pawnshop and pawned my ring. When I came back, we took a cab to Broadway and 145th Street, to the temporary housing-commission office. When I got there, I told one of the girls at the window that I wanted to write out a complaint against a tenement landlord.

She gave me a form to fill out and said I had to make out two copies. I sat down and started writing. It seemed like a whole lot to Mama, because Mama didn't do too much writing. She used a small sheet of paper even when she wrote a letter.

She kept bothering me while I was writing. She said, "Boy, what's all that you puttin' down there? You can't be saying nothin' that ain't the truth. Are you sure you know what you're talking about? Because I'm only complaining about the window, now, and it don't seem like it'd take that much writing to complain about just the one window."

"Mama, you're complaining about all the windows. Aren't all the windows in the same shape?"

"I don't know."

"Well, look here, Mama, isn't it cold in the whole house?"

"Yeah."

"When was the last time the windows were lined?"

"I don't know. Not since we lived in there."

"And you been livin' there seventeen years. Look, Mama, you got to do something."

"Okay, just don't put down anything that ain't true." She kept pulling on my arm.

"Look, Mama, I'm gonna write out this thing. When I finish, I'll let you read it, and if there's anything not true in it, I'll cross it out. Okay?"

"Okay, but it just don't seem like it take all that just to write out one complaint."

I had to write with one hand and keep Mama from pulling on me with the other hand. When I finished it, I turned in the two complaint forms, and we left. Mama kept acting so scared, it really got on my nerves. I said, "Look, Mama, you ain't got nothin' to be scared of."

She said she wasn't scared, but she just wanted to stay on the good side of the landlord, because sometimes she got behind in the rent.

"Yeah, Mama, but you can't be freezin' and catching colds just because sometimes you get behind in the rent. Everybody gets behind in the rent."

"Boy, I don't know what's wrong with you, but you're always ready to get yourself into something or start some trouble."

"Yeah, Mama, if I'm being mistreated, I figure it's time to start some trouble."

''Boy, I just hope to God that you don't get yourself into something one day that you can't get out of.''

After a couple of days, I asked Mama, ''What about the windows?''

''Nothin' about the windows.''

''What do you mean 'nothin' about the windows?'' I was getting a little annoyed, because she just didn't seem to want to be bothered. I said, ''You mean they didn't fix the windows yet? You didn't hear from the landlord?''

"No, I didn't hear from the landlord."

"Well, we're going back up to the housing commission."

"What for?"

"Because we're gon get something done about these windows."

"But something's already been done."

"What's been done, if you didn't hear anything from the landlord?"

"Some man came in here yesterday and asked me what windows."

"What man?"

"I don't know what man."

"Well, what did he say? Didn't he say where he was from?"

"No, he didn't say anything. He just knocked on the door and asked me if I had some windows that needed relining. I said 'yeah,' and he asked me what windows, so I showed him the three windows in the front."

"Mama, you didn't show him all the others?"

"No, because that's not so bad, we didn't need them relined."

"Mama, oh, Lord, why didn't you show him the others?"

"Ain't no sense in trying to take advantage of a good thing."

"Yeah, Mama. I guess it was a good thing to you."

I thought about it. I thought about the way Mama would go down to the meat market sometimes, and the man would sell her some meat that was spoiled, some old neck bones or some pig tails. Things that weren't too good even when they weren't spoiled. And sometimes she would say, "Oh, those things aren't too bad." She was scared to take them back, scared to complain until somebody said, "That tastes bad." Then she'd go down there crying and mad at him.

What Can Be Done?

You have now met some of America's poor. Each of them was one of the statistics in the data studied by the President's advisers.

The President delivered his message to Congress and asked for help for the poor. He said the whole nation should fight a "war on poverty."

Congress agreed and passed new laws designed to help the poor. Under these new laws, the government started new programs or enlarged old ones. These programs aimed to help poor people in many ways: by giving poor children a head start on their education before they entered first grade; by training men in new skills that would help them get jobs; by creating more jobs; by building houses and apartments that people with low incomes could afford; by giving poor people surplus food, or stamps that could be exchanged for food at stores; and by helping poor people get free legal and medical help.

The government started to fight so many different kinds of battles in its "war on poverty" because it knew that poverty is not one problem, but many. The laws passed by the government, however, were just a start. Congress set aside only a fraction of the money needed to wipe out poverty. But the new laws made many Americans aware, for the first time, that poverty was a problem in America.

There are still several million poor families in the United States. Different families are poor for different reasons, and some of them have not been reached by any of the plans for solving the poverty problem. But with each try, the problem-solvers learn more about the problem.

American technology produces enough food for everyone in the country. Now the problem is getting this food—along with a better standard of living—to everyone who needs it.

9

Technology: Problems and Solutions

Who Killed Gizzard Shad?

One day in November, the Public Health Service in Washington, D.C., received a message. More than 5 million dead fish were seen floating down the lower Mississippi River. Fish were being washed up along the shores of Venice, Louisiana. There were dead channel catfish, dead gizzard shad, dead fathead minnows, and dead menhaden.

Dead fish in Lake Michigan

"What killed the fish?" asked a person from the Public Health Service.

"We don't know," came the reply from Louisiana. "We tested the water, but found no good clues. We tested the water temperature, but our tests showed normal water temperature for the river."

Many fish cannot live in warm water or water that changes temperature very fast. Heated water is sometimes dumped into the river by factories along the Mississippi.

"We also tested the water for oxygen," the person from Louisiana reported. "Our tests showed plenty of oxygen in the river water."

Fish must get a good supply of oxygen from the water. Washing detergents use up the oxygen in a river. Detergents from washing dishes and clothes drain into the Mississippi from all the homes in the towns and cities along the river.

"It looks like you could use some help,"
offered the person from the Public Health Service.
"You can say that again! We have to find out
what is killing those fish."

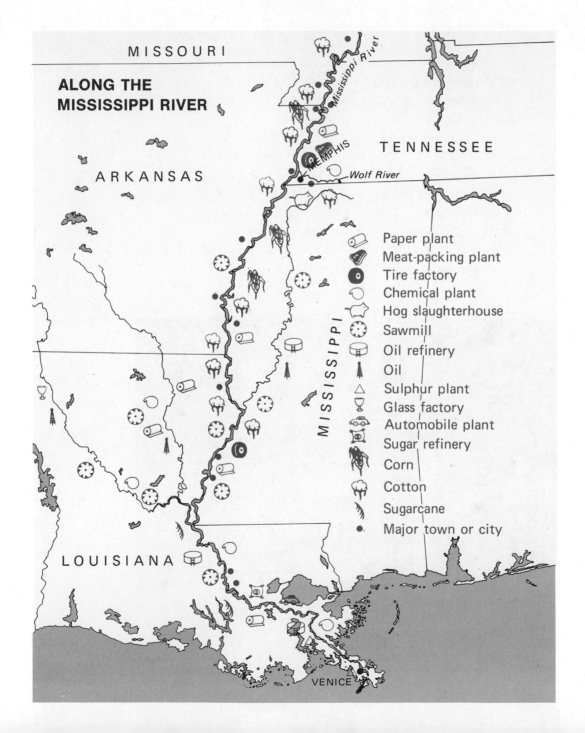

**ALONG THE
MISSISSIPPI RIVER**

MISSOURI

TENNESSEE

ARKANSAS

Mississippi River

MEMPHIS

Wolf River

Paper plant
Meat-packing plant
Tire factory
Chemical plant
Hog slaughterhouse
Sawmill
Oil refinery
Oil
Sulphur plant
Glass factory
Automobile plant
Sugar refinery
Corn
Cotton
Sugarcane
Major town or city

MISSISSIPPI

LOUISIANA

VENICE

THINKING OF IDEAS OR THEORIES

The Public Health Service sent a team of biologists to Louisiana to study the problem. The biologists searched for clues.

They saw that the dying fish did odd things. They jumped several feet out of the water when a boat moved through the water. Their bodies twisted and turned. Sometimes they landed on their backs and died.

The biologists also found traces of blood around the mouths and fins of the dead fish. They noticed that dying fish swam on the surface of the water and that dead fish floated on the surface of the water.

One hundred pounds of dead fish were packed in dry ice by the biologists. They also collected and froze some mud taken from the bottom of the Mississippi. Then they sent the fish and mud to their laboratories.

The biologists had several ideas or theories to explain why the fish had died. They could have died of starvation. They could have died of food poisoning or lead poisoning. Or they could have died from some kind of sickness.

Testing Theories

In the laboratory, the biologists tested the mud and the dead fish. These tests gave them more information. They used this information to test their theories. Which theories do you think explain why the fish died?

The biologists were fairly sure that the fish did not die of starvation. The Mississippi River had more than enough food to keep all of its fish alive. The biologists also believed that food or lead poisoning was not the killer. Laboratory tests turned up no trace of food or lead poisoning in the bodies of the dead fish. Tests also did not support the theory that the fish died from some sickness. Blood tests on the dead fish were normal. If the fish had been sick, their blood would not have tested normal. The biologists needed some new theories.

Could a bad storm have been the killer? Storm winds can rapidly cool a river's water, and sudden changes in water temperature kill fish. Investigators looked for clues to check out the storm theory. The Louisiana investigators had already checked the water temperature and said it was normal. There were no records of high winds or bad storms about the time the dead fish were found. The mystery was still unsolved.

Testing the Chemical Theory

The investigators tried another theory: An unknown chemical in the water or mud of the Mississippi could have killed the fish. Investigators tested the mud they had taken from the bottom of the Mississippi. They dropped some Mississippi mud into a tank of healthy fish. The fish twisted and turned. They turned over on their backs and died. There were traces of blood around their mouths and fins.

Investigators found out what chemicals were in the mud. They checked each one. They found small amounts of DDT and two other chemicals used to kill insects—dieldrin and endrin. Could one of these chemicals be the killer?

The biologists concentrated on endrin. They knew it could kill fish. But the Mississippi mud had only a very very small amount of endrin in it. In fact, there was only one-tenth of one part endrin to a million parts of mud. Could so little endrin cause the death of so many fish? The investigators were not sure.

Fish can store endrin in their systems. Little by little, the endrin builds up in the fish. When enough endrin is in their bodies, the fish begin to die.

The Public Health Service closed its investigation. Its report blamed the killing of gizzard shad on a chemical plant located 500 miles upstream from the scene of the crime. This plant made endrin and dumped its waste into a lake. There were small amounts of endrin in the waste. The waste and the endrin in it were carried down the Wolf River and into the Mississippi. To keep the endrin from getting into the Mississippi, the plant was ordered to stop dumping its waste into the lake.

Not everybody agreed with the Public Health Service. Some officials pointed out that endrin could get into the river in other ways. All along the Mississippi, endrin was used to spray crops and to keep mosquitoes and garden pests under control. The endrin could have washed off the fields into the river.

What do you think? What do you believe killed gizzard shad?

Controlling Insects

Few chemicals have been so widely used as DDT. It has helped protect crops from insects. It has brought diseases like malaria and sleeping sickness under control.

Now the miracle has been condemned. Long after the pests are dead, its critics say, DDT is active. It remains on small plants and in animals. They are eaten by larger animals, including people. Each one in turn absorbs the DDT. DDT does not lose its power to kill as it is passed from one victim to another.

THE PEST PROBLEM

One summer Egypt's cotton crop was attacked by cotton-leaf worms. Cotton is a very important crop in Egypt.

Losing the crop meant the loss of jobs for many Egyptians. There would be no work for those who harvested the cotton. There would be no work for those who hauled the cotton to the mills. There would be no work for those who prepared the cotton for use in the mills.

Egypt's merchants depend on the cotton crop, too. When there is little work in Egypt's cotton fields, there are fewer customers for Egypt's merchants. People with no money buy no goods.

When the cotton worms attacked, Egypt's government ordered the Egyptian people into the fields to pick the worms off the cotton plants by hand. More than a million men, women, and children left their jobs and classrooms for the fields. Worms threatened one and a half million acres of cotton.

For three hot summer months, the Egyptians lifted the worms and their eggs from the cotton plants.

DDT could have been sprayed on the cotton worms. That would have been quicker and more effective than handpicking. But people had learned that DDT was dangerous.

American farmers had sprayed their crops with DDT. Three years later, these farmers found dying birds. The birds had eaten worms that had eaten leaves sprayed with DDT.

Many people say that using DDT over a long period can harm birds, animals, and people. They have a lot of evidence.

But now food experts say that DDT and other pesticides must be used. If they are not used, they warn that the world's food supply may drop by as much as 50 percent. Food experts claim that pesticides are needed to produce more crops. Some day safer methods to control insects may be available.

ECOSYSTEMS

Your room, your house, your school are all part of the setting in which you live. All the things that surround you are part of your environment. The oxygen you breathe in and the carbon dioxide you breathe out are part of your environment.

Every living thing shares its environment with other living things. A community of animals, plants, and bacteria and the environment they share is called an ecosystem.

Living things within an ecosystem depend on one another. Plants produce the oxygen that animals breathe. Animals produce the carbon dioxide used by the plants. A healthy ecosystem is balanced. Everything produced by one part of the system will be used in another part of the system.

Ecosystems do not stand still. Sometimes their balance is attacked by natural things like droughts and floods. Sometimes human technology attacks the balance of an ecosystem.

Environments

Cars, trucks, and buses give off pollutants. In large cities there are a lot of cars, trucks, and buses. They give off more pollutants than the ecosystem can absorb.

Factories and power plants give off a great deal of smoke, steam, and chemical wastes. This pollution could destroy the ecosystem we live in.

A Case of Air Pollution

THE PITTSBURGH STORY

The city of Pittsburgh was one of the first
to face the problem of air pollution. The steel

industry was responsible for much of Pittsburgh's growth. But it also caused a large part of the city's pollution problem.

By 1940, doctors were saying that Pittsburgh was not a healthy place to live. Many people had lung diseases from breathing the smog over Pittsburgh. Industries found themselves unable to attract young, skilled workers to the city. Industries and people were leaving. Pittsburgh produced many useful goods, but who wanted to live there?

For years Pittsburgh had lived with the belief that smoke was good for the city. Soft, smoke-producing coal was cheap. It could be dug out of the hills overlooking the city. It could heat the homes of Pittsburgh's people. It could create jobs for many people.

Pittsburgh's steel mills used a lot of coal. In 1941 Europe was at war. There was a great demand for steel to build ships and tanks and guns. The mills kept busy day and night. Smoke belching out of Pittsburgh's smokestacks meant people were working. But Pittsburgh's air was heavy with soot.

Pittsburgh Attacks Its Problem

Three citizens decided it was time to campaign for smoke control. One was the editor of a local newspaper. Another was a doctor, the health director of the city of Pittsburgh. The third was a member of Pittsburgh's city council. The editor wrote editorials. The doctor spoke to business people and community groups. The council member introduced smoke control laws.

These three citizens told business people that businesses were leaving Pittsburgh and that they were taking jobs and customers with them. They told people that air pollution cost them money since it was harder to keep their clothes and homes clean. And they pointed out that Pittsburgh had become unhealthy and unattractive.

People wrote letters to local newspapers and to the city council asking for smoke control laws. Students painted posters showing how Pittsburgh would look if it were clean. Local merchants put the posters in their windows. A large number of clubs and community groups held meetings and urged their members to support the campaign for a clean Pittsburgh.

The people of Pittsburgh wore masks over their faces as part of a campaign for smoke control.

Cleaning the Air

In 1941 Pittsburgh's city council passed a smoke control law. It required everyone to use smokeless fuel or to use equipment that kept smoke from escaping into the air. But the law was not enforced until 1946.

By that time, David Lawrence was mayor of Pittsburgh. He had campaigned on a promise to clean up the city. One of the first things he did was to set up a smoke control board. The board sent inspectors to check on complaints. They looked at equipment and furnaces. And they made a few arrests.

Some of Pittsburgh's people were not happy with the mayor who enforced smoke control. Smokeless coal was more expensive than soft coal. There wasn't enough of it to supply all the people who wanted to buy it. The price was high. The equipment needed to burn the smokeless fuel was costly, too, and sometimes it broke down.

Pittsburgh also had another source of smoke to worry about. Factories outside the city limits were still operating without smoke control laws. The smoke from these factories drifted into Pittsburgh. The mayor took his fight to the state government.

He had the help of many of Pittsburgh's leaders. Richard King Mellon, a wealthy banker, worked hard for smoke control. He, and others working with him, made large profits from Pittsburgh's industries. Many of the mills they owned and controlled were the ones polluting Pittsburgh's air. As citizens, they wanted clean air. As millowners, many thought clean air would be too expensive.

Nevertheless, many of Pittsburgh's leaders banded together to fight for smoke control. Mellon, and the people working with him, convinced millowners that clean air was worth having even if it cost a lot to change to smokeless furnaces.

The mayor asked the state to pass a smoke control law. The state law would make railroads, as well as homes and industries outside the city limits, use smokeless fuels and smokeless furnaces.

The mayor waged a hard-hitting campaign for cleaner air. He made many enemies and many friends. He barely won the next election. But by 1950, Pittsburgh's air was cleaner.

Before and after smoke control

Pittsburgh Today

The city began to attract young, skilled workers. The city began to grow again. It tore down many of its old, ugly buildings and replaced them with new, modern buildings and parks. The city built a giant new sports stadium overlooking its three rivers.

In the 1970's Pittsburgh, along with other large American cities, was once again worrying about pollution. This time the exhaust from cars was the worst offender. Other sources included open fires and jet planes. Pittsburgh once again had an air pollution problem. What would you do about it if you lived in Pittsburgh?

10

Technology and the Future

Time

People think about time a lot. People have time. People do not have time. They are on time. They are not on time. School begins at a certain time. It ends at another. People's lives run on time.

THE CLOCK

The people who settled along the Nile River in Egypt made sundials to measure time. But not until much later, just about 500 years before Watt invented his steam engine, did men invent machines that recorded time more accurately. These machines were called clocks.

The first clocks used weights to turn a wheel that moved the hands of the clock. Later clocks used springs and pendulums to turn their wheels.

Many towns were so proud of having a
clock that they put it atop a church.

With a clock, people could divide a day into many even parts. One day had twenty-four hours. Each hour had sixty minutes, and each minute had sixty seconds. Can you imagine how clocks changed people's lives?

The clock also gave inventors ideas for other machines. Using the clock as a model, they developed other automatic machines based on the wheels and gears of the clock.

Philosophers used the idea of a clock to explain nature. They saw the universe as a giant clockwork. To them, the sun, stars, and planets worked together like a big machine.

By the time Watt's steam engine was in use in England, the clock was an important part of the lives of modern people. Their lives and their thoughts were shaped, in small ways and big ones, by the clock.

JAMES'S DIARY: 1848

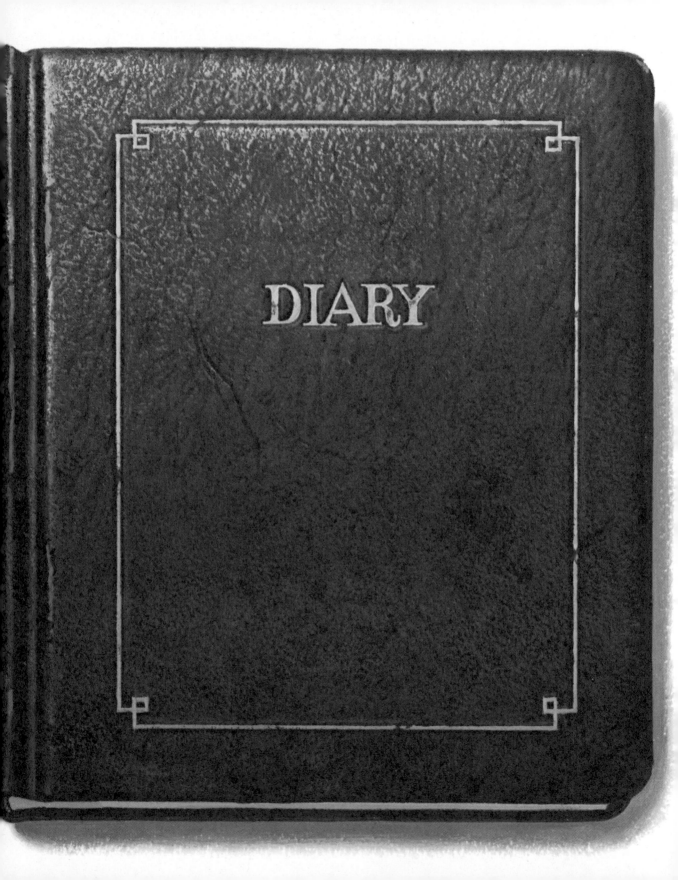

Feb. 3. 7:30 A.M. This diary belongs to James Whittaker of Milltown, Massachusetts. PRIVATE PROPERTY. Father and Mother gave me this diary for my birthday. I promised to write in it each morning before breakfast. Father gave me this advice: 1. The early bird catches the worm. 2. Always be on time. 3. Do my schoolwork very carefully and don't say anything unless I know what I'm talking about. 4. Think about what I want to be when I grow up and then work very hard to be it. Maybe I'll be like Father and keep the account books at the mill, because arithmetic is my best subject.

Feb. 4. 7:45 A.M. I must hurry and write because I'm late to breakfast. Yesterday was very exciting. A letter came from Boston by coach. Father read it to us at dinner. Aunt Mary and Uncle Walt and all our cousins are coming to visit for the month of June. I don't think I will like all my cousins staying here for a whole month, but they can't just come for one day — that would be a waste of time. Father said they may take me back to Boston with them. My first trip! Father also got a newspaper from the coachman and promised to read it aloud at breakfast today.

Feb. 5. 7:30 A.M. The newspaper said that the war with Mexico is over. Father talked with some other men about it last night, but I couldn't hear what they were saying. Father promised to tell me about it. I asked our teacher, but he said to pay attention to my Latin and forget about things happening far away in Mexico. I wonder what it's like in Mexico.

Feb. 6. 7:50 A.M. Must hurry again. My best friend Tom said his father knows a whole family from near here who are going out to California because there's gold out there. Father hasn't said anything about us going, and neither has Tom's father. Maybe it's not true about the gold. Anyway, Tom and I decided we wouldn't go unless we could go together. I wonder what it's like to leave your house and all your friends and relatives and go someplace new. I wonder what it's like in California.

Feb. 7. 8:00 A.M. Mother just came in and looked like she was going to holler at me for being late to breakfast. But when she saw me writing she went away. Yesterday was wash day, and now that it's over, I guess she's in a good mood. It must be hard to be grown up, because you have to do the same jobs over and over again. Father has been very busy at the mill and goes to bed soon after dinner, so he hasn't had a chance to tell me about Mexico yet. Maybe he will on Sunday, when we go for our walk after church.

Feb. 8.   7:00 A.M. Today is Sunday and I have to dress for church. Yesterday Tom and I were playing in that swamp where we're not supposed to go. We were just pretending that it was California and we were digging for gold. But that Mrs. Beedle came by the road and saw us. She said she'd tell our parents. Every time I fidget in church she turns around and stares at me like her eyes were darts. I hope she won't be at church today, but I just know she will. I feel like those dart-looks of hers will be around for the rest of my life. Father says they are building a lot of railroads now. Maybe I'll be a railroad engineer so I won't have to be looked at by Mrs. Beedle every time I do something wrong. The only good thing about today is my walk with father, so he can answer all my questions about Mexico, California, and my trip to Boston this summer. I guess this is going to be an exciting year.

Aquanauts living underwater

My Ambition !!!
We were <u>right near here</u> on our vacation last spring! Have to think of a way to make this my science project this term

Mary - My best friend when I lived in Dayton, Ohio

Rachel - My best friend when I lived in Detroit.

My best friend Ann Milltown, Mass.

WRITE Letters! (air mail)

Very good ecology program on TV. Science
project???? Things to look for on class
ecology walk next month:
- birds
- insects
- plants
- Streams (polluted?)
- air pollution
- trash to collect

War

I asked Daddy and Mommy about the war in Vietnam.
They said there are lots of books being written about it
now that it was over. They told me the library had lots
of magazines and books with things about the
Vietnam War in them. Could this be my class report??

Answer LETTERS!

Spring vacation: Visit Aunt Susan
　　　　　　　Los Angeles
　　　　　　Trips to Boston
　　　　　with mom?
(Botanical Gardens... science
project ???)
(See a play?)
(tour of a Tv Station)

← My Ambition

Programs to be sure not
to miss this week:
6 o'clock news (every
night)
Charlie Brown special (mon.)
Wizard of Oz (wed.)
Heart transplant
special (Thurs.)

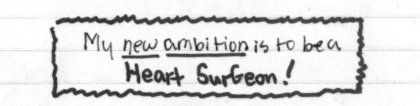

My _new_ _ambition_ is to be a
Heart Surgeon!

✭✭✭ Anne is moving to California!! ✭✭✭
Her father works in an electronics plant and is changing
jobs to a company in Los Angeles. I don't feel _too_
bad because maybe I can visit her when I go
visit Aunt Susan. I guess Janet and I will be best
friends now. Janet says Charlie Brown is silly! We
watch the horror movie together on Saturdays.

This is _definitely_ my new ambition unless I
become a foreign correspondent for a newspaper. It's awfully hard to decide!

Machines that Help People Think

Some technology, like the wheel, the steam engine, and the electric power-tool, extended the work people can do with their bodies. Some technology expanded the work people can do with their minds. The numbering system used by the people of Shang China helped them to keep government records and to figure out how to make bronze. Later, people invented ways to help them work with numbers.

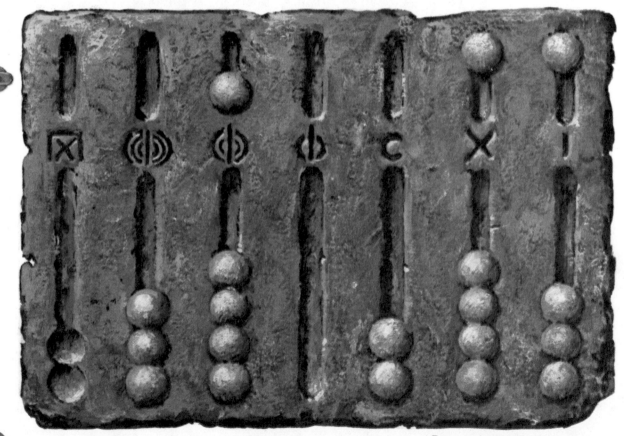

Roman hand abacus

THE ABACUS

To help them count, the Romans improved on an ancient invention—the abacus. They carved grooves into a bronze plaque and fitted little balls into each groove.

The seven long grooves across the bottom of the abacus and the seven short grooves at the top are like the columns you put numbers in. Starting from the right, like columns, the long grooves stand for ones, tens, hundreds, thousands, 10 thousands, 100 thousands, and millions. In the long grooves, each ball stands for a ten or a hundred, depending on its groove. In the short grooves, each ball stands for a five-group: five ones, five tens, five hundreds, and so on to five millions. Only balls moved up or down to the center of the abacus are counted. Here is the number 6,124 on the abacus:

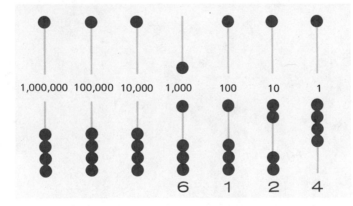

Romans could only do simple sums on this abacus. To add, they kept the second number in their head and added it to the first number on the abacus.

The Chinese used an abacus with bamboo rods as counters perhaps as early as 600 B.C. Many people still use the abacus today, among them the Chinese, the Japanese, and the Russians.

CALCULATING MACHINES

As bigger and better machines were built people could add, subtract, multiply, and divide faster and more accurately. Some of these machines were mechanical. Others were powered by electricity.

COMPUTERS

In 1943 a new machine was added to people's technology. The first real computer that worked was built in that year. It was called the Mark I, and it was a lot bigger than an abacus or an adding machine. It weighed almost two tons. It contained 530 miles of wire, 1,210 ball bearings, and had 765,299 parts.

Powered by electricity, the Mark I used mechanical switches to start and stop the flow of electricity. According to one writer, all those clicking switches made Mark I at work sound like a roomful of people knitting. Despite the noise, it could do three additions per second.

In 1946 ENIAC was built. By this time, faster ways to turn the flow of electricity on and off had been discovered. ENIAC was able to do 4,500 additions per second.

ENIAC was invented by a person who worried about what the weather would be like. The people of Shang China had tried to find out about the weather from oracle bones. The person who invented ENIAC thought he could predict the weather better if he had a machine to help him. He was right.

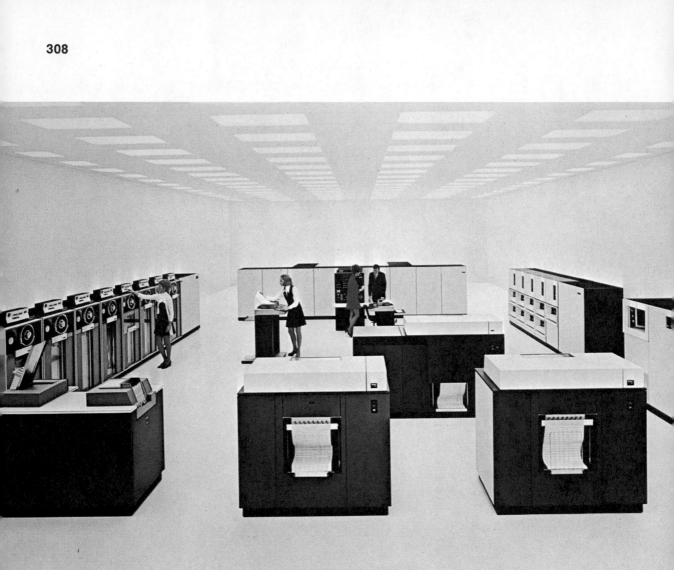

Today's computers work faster than ever.
A computer today can do more than a million
additions per second.

What the Computer Can Do

Once you give a computer information, it
can store that information and remember it forever.
It can use this information whenever you ask
it to. It can figure very very fast. And it can do
the same job over and over again without getting
tired or bored.

Computers can do many different kinds
of jobs. Here are just a few of the jobs they can do:
guide spacecraft to the moon; sell tickets to
concerts, plays, and baseball games; design
airplanes; place telephone calls; match jobs and
job-seekers; make out report cards; drive trains and
planes; and solve complicated problems.

How a Computer Works: Programming

Computers need exact instructions to do
a job. You can show people how to tie a shoe,
and by watching and copying you, they, too, can tie a
shoe. But you have to tell a computer every
move it is going to make. And you have to tell it in
language it can understand. Giving the computer
the instructions it needs to do a job is called
programming the computer. Programming a
computer sharpens your thinking and forces you to be
more precise.

Before you can program a computer, you have to figure out every step that must be taken to solve your problem. Suppose you wanted to program a computer to direct traffic on a lonely country road.

Road A

Sometimes children cross Road A to go to school and back. You want a traffic light to tell them when it is safe to cross. The traffic light can be timed to change from red to green or from green to red every few seconds. But at most times of the day no one will be crossing the road. Children will be crossing the road to go to and from school only at certain times of the day. What instructions would you give to a person you were training to run the traffic light? What instructions would you give a computer that was going to run the traffic light?

People's Partnership with the Computer

Some people think that computers might control people's work some day. They forget that a computer can only do what it is told to do.

When Apollo 11 was just about ready to land the first astronauts on the moon, their computer suddenly started announcing that it didn't know what to do. It was getting new data that it hadn't been programmed to handle. The astronauts had to make the actual landing without the help of the computer. But they did need the computer to get them from the earth to the moon in the first place.

DIVIDING WORK BETWEEN
PEOPLE AND COMPUTERS

Early humans seldom specialized. Individuals built their own shelter, hunted for their own food, and fought their enemies themselves. But as people began to modernize, they also began to specialize more. Today, modern people tend to specialize. Some are architects, some are cooks, some are soldiers. And even these jobs are divided. Some architects design only shopping centers or churches. Some cooks make only pastry. A soldier might be a pilot, a welder, or a radio operator.

One reason people specialized was that knowledge grew. Today, no single person can hold in his head all the information needed to build an office building or a jet plane. The president of a construction company or of an airplane manufacturing company depends upon engineers and other specialists for information and advice.

The computer is taking over many of these specialized jobs. Here are some of the specialized jobs a computer can do:

A computer attached to a typewriter can remember a student's past skills in arithmetic, plan a lesson just for her, grade her work, and print out, "VERY GOOD, HELEN. SEE YOU MONDAY."

A computer can do millions of engineering calculations for an architect's firm.

As people write instructions to program computers, they think through the steps so thoroughly that they find new ways to break up jobs. Greater specialization takes place. New computers able to do these highly specialized jobs are developed. Computers could take over more and more jobs once done by people.

In busy police stations, computers help police record and answer emergency calls.

Computers help industries keep track of such things as costs, sales, and inventory. This computer produces data in response to the human voice.

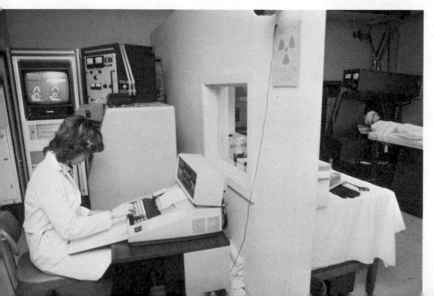

The ACTA-Scanner, a computerized X-ray machine, helps physicians diagnose diseases.

Courtesy of the Digital Information Science Corporation

Technology and the Quality of Life

THE IMPACT OF TECHNOLOGY

How can you decide whether changes caused by technology are good or bad? How can you forecast whether technology will create more problems than it solves?

Suppose a textile mill creates jobs for many people and produces beautiful cloth at a low cost. But at the same time it pollutes a nearby river. Has the textile mill created more problems than it has solved? How do you decide?

Suppose the space industry creates many jobs and many new products. But people employed in the space industry often have to move quickly from job to job and from place to place. Their families never have a chance to make close friends. Has the space industry created more problems than it has solved? How do you decide?

In the past, people have developed technology without very much thought about how it would be used and controlled. Now people are realizing the price they could pay if they fail to think about the problems technology creates.

Economists have ways to measure changes in a nation's economy. These measures are called economic indicators. The rate at which unemployment is increasing or decreasing is an economic indicator.

Economists measure this rate. They also
watch to see if prices are rising. They measure
a nation's output of goods and services, too. By
watching economic indicators such as these,
economists can make suggestions that help create
jobs when they are needed, help control prices,
and help encourage the production of goods.

Some people think nations must also measure
social conditions. Social indicators would help to
do this. Social indicators would help people
know if schools are doing their job. They would
tell how technology is changing people's lives. They
would measure pollution and help people predict
what might happen if pollution isn't controlled. As
one government official said, social indicators
would tell "whether the country is more liveable
from year to year."

DESIGNING THE FUTURE

R. Buckminster Fuller is an architect, an
inventor, and a thinker about people's uses of
technology. He said this about making the
future more liveable:

Birds build nests and every one of them is a superb
piece of design. But the same species of bird will
always build exactly the same nest. There is no change
in design except by man, and he is always and quite
rapidly changing the type of nest he builds.

It is a very responsible matter to change the
environment. When people alter the environment and
pollute, they're not being responsible. We have to
see how very irresponsible we've been.

I once visited one of the big copper companies
(which also handled nickel and tin) and coming out

of its smokestack were fumes that were worth perhaps $700 a day. But the actual cost of recovering them was just a little more than the $700. Because the company found they wouldn't make any money by recovering them, valuable metals were just going off in the sky, landing as dust around New York City.

This, to me, is a design challenge. That's the kind of thing I really care about.

ARTISTS LOOK AT TODAY

The City, *Fernand Leger*

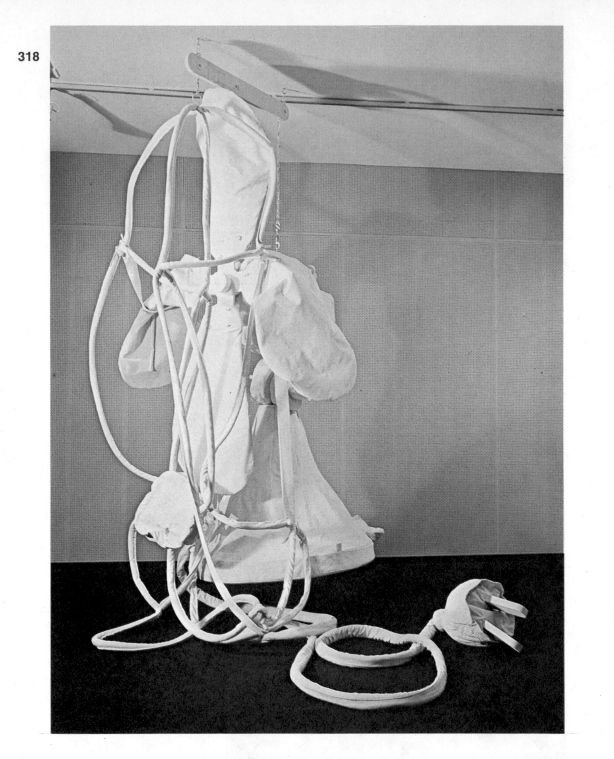

Giant Soft Fan, Ghost Version, *Claes Oldenburg*

F. M. Variant, *Ernest Trova*

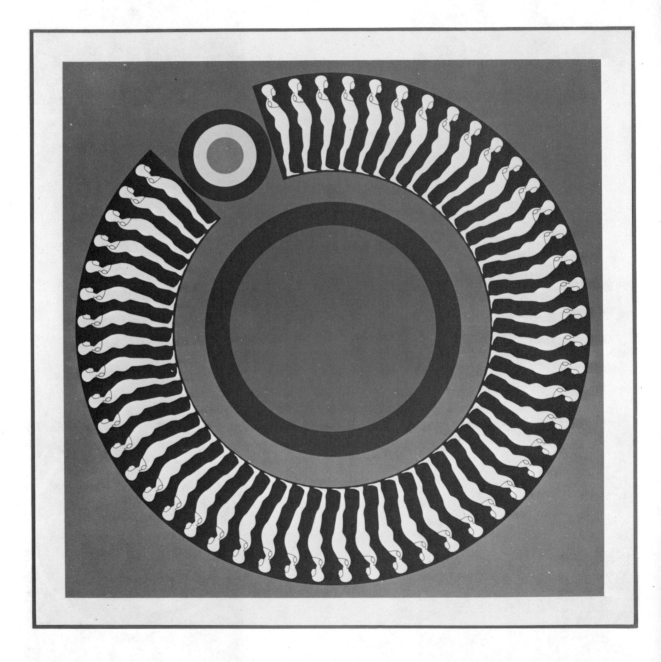

Numbers,
Robert Indiana

SIX

SEVEN

EIGHT

NINE

ZERO

YOUR DESIGN FOR THE FUTURE

Many people today talk about the quality of life—the good things and bad things in the way people live. Improving the quality of life means making many hard choices.

People must decide what to do with the technology and other resources available to them. Should the United States use its technology and other resources to develop and to build a supersonic airplane? Should it use its technology and other resources to rebuild its cities? Should the United States use its technology and other resources to explore the moon? Should it use its technology and other resources to clean up its air and water and to protect areas not yet polluted?

The choices you make will affect the quality of your life. How would you use technology to help design the future?

It is for you to decide how you will use the talents and the technology available to you. Your decision will affect the quality of your life and the life of every other living thing.

Glossary

FULL PRONUNCIATION KEY

The pronunciation of each word is shown just after the word, in this way: **ab bre vi ate** (ə brē′ vē āt). The letters and signs used are pronounced as in the words below. The mark ′ is placed after a syllable with primary or heavy accent, as in the example above. The mark ′ after a syllable shows a secondary or lighter accent, as in **ab bre vi a tion** (ə brē′ vē ā′ shən).

a	hat, cap	k	kind, seek	u	cup, butter
ā	age, face			ù	full, put
ä	father, far	l	land, coal	ü	rule, move
		m	me, am		
b	bad, rob	n	no, in		
ch	child, much	ng	long, bring	v	very, save
				w	will, woman
d	did, red	o	hot, rock		
		o	open, go	y	young, yet
e	let, best	ô	order, all		
ē	equal, be	oi	oil, voice	z	zero, breeze
ėr	term, learn	ou	house, out	zh	measure, seizure
f	fat, if	p	paper, cup		
g	go, bag	r	run, try	ə represents:	
h	he, how	s	say, yes	a in about	
		sh	she, rush	e in taken	
i	it, pin	t	tell, it	i in April	
ī	ice, five	th	thin, both	o in lemon	
j	jam, enjoy	ᵺ	then, smooth	u in circus	

abacus (ab′ ə kəs), a set of beads used for counting and arithmetic (302)

adobe (ə do′ bē), a building material made of clay and straw dried in the sun (155)

Amazon (am′ ə zän), the jungle region surrounding the Amazon River in South America (108)

Andes (an′ dēz), a chain of mountains more than 4,000 miles long, in western South America (100)

anthropologist (an thrə päl′ ə jist), a scientist who studies human life (147)

Anyang (än yäng′), a city in central China which once was the capital of the Shang kingdom (33)

Appalachia (ap ə lā′ chə), the region of the eastern United States that surrounds the Appalachians (240)

Appalachians (ap ə lā′ chənz), a mountain range in the eastern United States (241)

archeologist (är kē äl′ ə jəst), a scientist who studies the remains of people who lived long ago (6)

Aztecs (az′ tekz), a people who lived in Mexico and founded a great empire (158)

baba (bä′ bä), the Kikuyu word for father (128)

Bocanegra, Angel (bōk ə nä′ grə, än′ hel), a Mexican aviator who helped to found a school in his village of Tepoztlan (180)

broker (brō′ kər), a person employed by sellers or buyers of goods to conduct their business dealings (200)

bronze (bronz), a metal made from mixing tin and copper that is stronger and harder than either tin or copper alone (35)

Brown, Claude, a writer best known for *Manchild in the Promised Land,* a book about his experiences growing up in Harlem (245)

calligraphy (kə lig′ rə fē), the art of beautiful hand-writing (39)

carding, preparing fibers for spinning by cleaning or combing them with a toothed tool or wire brush (56)

Cara (kar′ ə), a people of Ecuador (107)

Census Bureau, an office of the government of the United States which collects information about the American population (229)

Chengchow (jung jō′), a city in China which may once have been the capital of the Shang kingdom (35)

Cheops (kē′ äpz), a ruler of ancient Egypt who lived around 2600 B.C. Cheops is sometimes known as Khufu. (19)

clan (klan), a group of several households that claim they are descended from a common ancestor (120)

Cortez, Hernando (kôr tez′, er nän′ dō), the Spanish conqueror of Mexico. Cortez was born in 1485 and died in 1547. (166)

cottage industry, manufacturing done in people's homes, for example, textile-making in England in the 1700's (51)

Cuernavaca (kwer nə vä′ kə), a city in Mexico (171)

Cuzco (küz′ kō), a city in Peru, once the capital of the Inca empire (99)

DDT, an abbreviation for dichloro-diphenyl-trichloro-ethane, a powerful substance used to kill insects. Until recently, DDT was the chemical used most often for spraying crops in the United States. (264)

Defoe, Daniel, an English writer (1660–1731) best known for his novels, *Robinson Crusoe* and *Moll Flanders* (54)

Diaz, Porfirio (dē′ äz, pôr fēr′ ē ō), the president of Mexico from 1876 to 1880 and from 1884 to 1911 (176)

Dickens, Charles, an English author who was born in 1812 and died in 1870 (64)

diviner (də vīn′ ər), a person who tries to foresee the future (37)

Dolores (dō lôr′ ās), a town in Mexico (173)

dragon bones, ancient bones, covered with writing, found in China. These bones used to be ground up and sold as medicine. (33)

dynasty (dī′ nə stē), a succession of rulers from the same family (33)

ecology (ē käl′ ə jē), the science that deals with the relationships of living things (298)

economist (ē kän′ ə məst), a scientist who studies the ways goods are produced and used (212)

ecosystem (ek′ ō sis təm), the interaction between a group of living things and their environment (269)

endrin (en′ drin), a chemical used to kill insects. (264)

engineer (en′ jə nir′), a scientist that makes things found in nature useful to humankind (20)

environment (en vī′ rə mənt), surroundings. When used in ecology, environment can mean the surroundings found in nature, not those created by people. (269)

exchange, a place where buyers and sellers, or their brokers, meet to conduct their business (198)

fachalina (fä chä lē′ nə), a headcloth woven by the Indians of Otavalo. It is usually made of blue and white cotton. (110)

Fuller, R. Buckminster, an American architect, inventor, and engineer (316)

futures contract, an agreement to buy a certain amount of a product that will be delivered at a specific date in the future (200)

geologist (jē ol′ ə jist), a scientist who deals with the history of the earth as recorded in rocks (8)

Gikuyu (ge kō′ yō), an African tribe in Kenya. The name is also spelled Kikuyu. (123)

Grito de Dolores (grē′ tō dä dō lôr′ ās), the name of a rallying cry of the Mexican revolution (173)

hacienda (äs ē en′ də), a large estate in a Spanish-speaking country (105)

hand ax, a simple stone tool made by early humans (8)

Hershey, a town in Pennsylvania, the location of the Hershey Foods Corporation (192)

Hidalgo, Miguel (ē däl′ gō, mē gel′), a Mexican priest (1753–1811) who started a revolt against Spain's rule of Mexico (173)

hieroglyphics (hī rō glif′ ikz), a system of writing that uses pictures as symbols; also, the writing developed in ancient Egypt (24)

Homo habilis (hō′ mō hab′ il is), a type of early being who made tools (10)

Horus (hō′ rus), the ancient Egyptian god of light and heaven, often shown as a man with the head of an ibis (31)

ideogram (id′ ē ə gram), a writing symbol that stands for an idea (23)

Imhotep (im hō′ tep), an architect in ancient Egypt who designed the first step pyramid (18)

Incas (ing′ kəz), a people who founded a great empire in South America (99)

income (in′ kum), benefit gained from capital or labor that is usually measured in money (212)

Indiana, Robert, an American artist (320)

irrigation (ir ə gā′ shən), using technology to supply land with water (31)

Juarez, Benito (wä′ rez, ben ē′ tō), the first Indian president of Mexico. He was born in 1806 and died in 1872. (175)

Kenyatta, Jomo (ken yä′ tə, jō′ mō), the first president of Kenya (124)

Kere-Nyaga (kir′ ē-nī äg′ ə), the Kikuyu name for Mount Kenya (123)

kersie (ker′ zē), a heavy wool or wool and cotton cloth used to make work clothes, uniforms, and coats (56)

kihongoye (kē hun gō′ yə), the Kikuyu word for nosey (130)

Kikuyu (ki kō′ yō), an African tribe whose home is in central Kenya. The name is also spelled Gikuyu. (98)

Kyoto (kyō′ tō), one of the largest cities in Japan (69)

Lawrence, David, a mayor of Pittsburgh who did much to clean up the city's air (279)

Leakey, Louis S. B. (lē′ kē), an archeologist who discovered the remains of early life in Africa (2)

Leakey, Mary, an archeologist who discovered the remains of early life in Africa (2)

Lewis, Oscar, an American anthropologist best known for his studies of Mexican villagers and Puerto Ricans in San Juan and New York (156)

lignite (lig′ nīt), a type of soft coal used for fuel (115)

living floor, the remains of a site that served as a home for early humans (7)

Ludd, Ned, the leader of the Luddites in England in the early 1800's. The Luddites were textile workers who protested violently against the lower wages and poor quality of textiles which they felt were a result of the new textile machines. (60)

Madero, Francisco (mä dêr′ ō, frän sis′ kō), one of the leaders of the Mexican revolution of 1910, and briefly, president of Mexico (178)

maito (mī′ tō), the Kikuyu word for mother (128)

Manchester (man′ ches tər), the fourth largest city in England (62)

Martinez, Pedro (mär tē′ nez, pā′ drō), an imaginary name given by Oscar Lewis to a Tepoztlan peasant he wrote about (156)

mastaba (mas′ tə bə), an early type of tomb built in ancient Egypt (17)

material culture, all the different types of goods used by a group of people (156)

Matsui (mat sü′ ē), a Japanese family name (74)

Mellon, Richard King, a wealthy Pittsburgh banker (280)

metate (me tä′ tā), a stone slab and roller used for grinding corn (161)

Mexico City, the capital of Mexico, built on the site of the ancient Aztec capital, Tenochtitlan (148)

Mogai (mō gī′), a Kikuyu word meaning God (123)

Mogo wa Kebiro (mō′ gō wä kē bir′ ō), a prophet in a Kikuyu tale (136)

monsoon (män sün′), a seasonal wind that brings heavy rains to India and Southeast Asia (221)

Montezuma (män tə zü′ mə), the Aztec emperor at the time Cortez conquered Mexico (158)

moro (môr′ ō), a Kikuyu word meaning son of (128)

Mount Imbabura (im bä bü′ rə), an inactive volcano, over 15,000 feet high, in the Andes of Ecuador (107)

Mount Kenya (ken′ yə), an inactive volcano, over 17,000 feet high, in central Kenya (123)

Mukundan, Mooliyil (mü kun dän′, mü′ lē yil), an agricultural expert in India (222)

munyinyi (mü nē ē′ nē), a Kikuyu word meaning little (133)

mware (mwär′ ē), a Kikuyu word meaning daughter of (128)

myth (mith), a story used by people to explain events in nature or history (30)

Nairobi (nī rō′ bē), the capital of Kenya (124)

Newcomen, Thomas, an English inventor (1663–1729) who developed one of the first steam engines (47)

Ngai (ngī), a Kikuyu word meaning God (137)

Nile, the longest river in Africa, flowing from Lake Victoria to the Mediterranean Sea (15)

nyoni ya nyagathanga (nī ō' nē-yä-nī äg əth än' gə), a Kikuyu name for a type of small bird (135)

Oldenburg, Claes, a Swedish-born American artist (318)

Omechtli (o mech' tlī), a Mexican Indian name (161)

oracle bones, another name for the "dragon bones" of China (37)

Orasac (ôr' ə shätz), a village in Serbia in Yugoslavia (115)

Osaka (ō sä' kə), the second largest city in Japan (84)

Osiris (ō sī' ris), the ancient Egyptian god of the dead (30)

Otavalo (ō tä vä' lō), a town in Ecuador on the slopes of Mount Imbabura (107)

Owen, Robert, an English millowner who worked for better factory conditions. He was born in 1771 and died in 1858. (53)

phonogram (fō' nō gram), a writing symbol that stands for a sound (24)

pictogram (pik' tō gram), a writing symbol that is simply a picture of the object it represents (23)

pollution (pə lü' shən), dirtying and introducing unwholesome things into the environment (273)

poncho (pän' chō), a square of cloth with a slit in the middle for the head, used as a cloak (107)

poverty level, a minimum annual income below which people are considered to live in poverty (237)

pyramid (pir' ə mid), a structure with a square base and four triangular walls which meet at the top (15)

pyrethrum (pī rē' thrəm), a type of flower used to make insecticides (141)

Quauhtli (kwät' lē), a Mexican Indian name (158)

Quechua (kech' wə), a language spoken by the Incas and several other groups of South American Indians (98)

Quetzalcoatl (ket säl kwät' əl), a god of the Aztecs (165)

resources (rē sôrs′ əz), available means or wealth. Resources are usually divided by economists into natural resources (forests, minerals, land, water, etc.); capital resources (the machinery and money that can be used to make new wealth); and human resources (the labor of people ready, willing, and able to work).

rurales (rü rä′ lās), a special police force made up of ex-bandits, started by Porfirio Diaz in Mexico (176)

scribe, an official whose job involves writing and keeping records (21)

Serbia (sər′ bē ə), a region of Yugoslavia (115)

shalloon (sha lün′), a lightweight wool used to line coats and uniforms (56)

Shang, the name of a ruling dynasty of ancient China (13)

spinning jenny, a machine used for spinning wool or cotton (48)

squatter (skwot′ ər), a person who settles on land without owning it or paying rent for it (140)

standard of living, a term used in economics to refer to the variety and number of goods necessary to maintain a particular way of life (212)

subsistence economy (səb sis′ təns ē kän′ə mē), a system of livelihood that is not based on money (107)

subsistence farming, a system of farming in which people produce only enough goods to support themselves. They usually do not have surplus goods to sell. (141)

supply and demand, a term used by economists. Supply refers to the different quantities of a particular good or service that would be offered for sale at various prices at a particular time. Demand refers to the different quantities of a particular good or service that would be purchased at various prices at a particular time. (205)

Tanjore (tan jôr′), a region of India also called Thanjavur (222)

Taxco (täs′ kō), a city in Mexico (171)

Index

Art Credits

Richard Amundsen—122–123, 132, 146–147, 157, 160, 171, 188, 301

Hal Ashmead—55

Delores Bego—96–97

Judith M. Craig—146, 158, 180

Danmark and Michaels, Inc.—16, 36, 44, 99, 112, 125, 167, 192–193, 241, 260

Monroe Eisenberg—11, 43, 61, 63, 95, 145, 191, 207, 225, 257, 283

Bill George—42, 45, 113, 190, 212, 250–251, 297, 323

Robert Goldstein—1, 2–3, 4–5, 6, 226, 238, 255, 289, 290–300

Fred Harsh—231, 232, 263

Kardwell Associates—223

Joanne Scribner—236–237, 314–315

Robert Van Nutt—138–139

Ed Vebell—12–13, 136–137

Vantage Art, Inc.—47, 98, 127, 192, 208, 218–219, 233–234

Photo Credits